Write Like You Don't Need the Money

A compilation of *Off the Cuff* columns
by Sharon Marie – she is
the daughter of Betty
Brouthers & I have
loved her columns over
the years – enjoy! :)

Printed in the United States of America.

Booklocker.com, Inc.
2003

Write Like You Don't Need the Money

Sharon Kuhn Young

Kelli,

So you've got a husband — a mom + a husband — you will be able to relate completely! :) I hope you read something that makes you smile!

Sharon

Special thanks to….

My readers…for being so faithful;
My publishers...Kathleen Ballanfant and Dick Williams... for their
    constant support and encouragement;
Anita and Michael Brown of cowboychuck.com...for sharing their
    talent in a wonderful, random act of kindness;
My Thursday night friends…for lovingly holding the mirror;
Joe "Giuseppe" Foster, my Copy Editor and sweet friend...
    who said "Yes" and got more than he bargained for!

My family, for believing in me...

Hugh Young (husband Hugh), Champ (our dog), Betty (my
Mom) and Jay Brouthers, Milton (my Dad) and Suzie Kuhn.
My siblings, their spouses and my beloved nieces and nephews...
Tommy and Marsha (sister), Mark and Paul Williams; Brent and
Diane (sister), David, Jonathan and Julia Rager; Jeffrey (brother),
Cynthia, Alicia and Kristen Kuhn; Paul, Camille (sister by
marriage), Hannah, and Laurel Christopher and J.P., our littlest
angel.

**And to my precious friends, who have always been
family too…**

Dedication

To Moses Mibiru, because I'll always love you
"a bushel and a peck" and to all the children of Uganda
who taught me about joy

Partial proceeds of this book will be donated to Uganda
Children's Charity Foundation (www.uccf.org); an
organization committed to the future of the AIDS orphans in
Uganda, Africa

About the Author

Sharon (Marie) Kuhn Young has a full time "real job" and writes a slice of life humor column once a week from Atlanta, Georgia. Born in Buffalo, NY and raised in Houston, Texas, Sharon wanted to be a journalist but her father advised her that there was no money in it. So, she got her BBA and proceeded to make no money for eighteen years as a political fundraiser instead. She is a Texas Aggie, a former Peace Corp Volunteer, a Kappa, a Methodist, a Republican, a daughter, a wife, a sister and a friend. This qualifies her to write about nothing or everything depending on how you see it. Her toughest job ever was waiting tables and she does not knowingly associate with bad tippers.

You can contact Sharon via her website:
www.sharonmarie.com

Table of Contents

Introduction

The cartoon woman on the cover is me, or I am her - - whichever. For the likeness to be complete the following minor alterations would need to be made:

- My dog Champ would be asleep on top of the pile of papers on the floor;
- The plant on the filing cabinet would be dead;
- The trash can would be empty because I compulsively empty trash;
- There would be multiple smaller piles of paperwork with sticky notes on each that I'm ignoring as opposed to the one large pile;
- I would be in shorts and a t-shirt, certainly never a dress;
- My short blonde hair would be in a one-inch ponytail;
- The coffee would be spilling on me, not the floor. I try not to go anywhere without a stain on my blouse;
- The print cartridge in the printer not depicted in this scene would be out of black ink;
- The desk phone would be cordless and…
- I'd be talking on my cell because to call someone back on the free line makes too much sense.

This is how I feel most days. I'm not convinced that I thrive on chaos but certainly I prefer it since I've done nothing to simplify my life over the last two decades.

It is from this place that I write my column so you can see why I call it *Off the Cuff*. Welcome to my world! I hope you read something that makes you smile.

Sharon Marie

Hair Bonnet Liberation

Some people dream of having enough money to travel the world, buy jewels, and shop forever. Me? *I dream of having enough money to hire someone to come in and blow-dry my hair every morning!!* Can you relate, when I say after thirty-plus years of shampooing and styling my hair, I am just over it? I mention this because, just yesterday, I received an electric, round brush for my birthday from my sweet friend, Nancy. If the brush had only arrived with my hairdresser, Phillip, attached...it would have been "The Perfect Gift".

Blow-drying your hair appears, on the surface, to be such a simple chore. I try to blame my disdain for this ritual on the fact I have thick hair. I think the truth is - - I am just plain lazy. I have mornings when I stand in front of the mirror with a swami towel wrapped around my head, thinking perhaps we dismissed the whole beauty parlor thing a little too soon.

As a side bar for anyone under thirty years old - - beauty parlors became salons about the same time noodles became pasta.

I giggled for years about the notion of women running to a beauty parlor once a week...to have their hair frozen into place. I mean, how could anyone think of having the same hair-do, day-in and day-out? Where was the creativity and freedom in that? How could women of my Mother's generation allow their entire social existence to be invisibly linked to when they were getting their hair "done"?

Even loyal fans of the "tease and freeze" look will admit that, by day seven, it is time for a wash and comb-out. I looked in the mirror this morning. The options were either hiding my limp hair under a baseball cap or suffering through my AM ritual. I realized once again...my Mother and her peers are very wise women.

Let's ignore the hair itself. Let's take a look at the residual benefits of having one's hair "done". Beauty parlors are a husband- and children-"free zone", the benefits of which are too obvious to mention. These women don't sit there worrying about what their hair is going to look like! They already know! So it is ***stress-free time.***

They don't have to purchase ten kinds of shampoo/conditioner/gel/ mousse/spray, so I'm certain it is also a money-saver. Most importantly, these women do not have to hold both arms above their head for thirty minutes every morning, looking like monkeys, while switching out three kinds of brushes, to achieve the right look. ***Boy, did my generation teach these women a thing or two about what it is to be liberated!***

We didn't move immediately into the wash-and-blow phase. We had ten years of bonnet dryers and spongy curlers, to ease us into the notion good-hair-days had their price. We left the bonnets for the shag look. This has all of us looking at old pictures, wondering, what we were thinking. Finally, thanks to Dorothy Hammel, women bought into the lie that short hair was easier to style. It is in this great untruth that we remain today!

Epilogue: So here's my question. What, what is so liberating about being attached to a dryer with a cord five feet long...***when you don't have any hands free anyway? Does anyone still have a bonnet they would be willing to sell me?***

Half an Earring is NOT Better than One!

My car could be stolen or I could be robbed of all my worldly possessions but **nothing *crawls under my skin like losing just one earring!***

True story - - I was flying on business to San Antonio, Texas. I have inherited my Father's ability to nod off in any mode of transport. I had been in deep REM sleep since we took off. I wake up slowly, I yawn, I run my fingers through my hair, and I conduct the unconscious check for my earrings as I always do.

My left earring has disappeared! No, not just the earring back which can be temporarily remedied with tape, Band-Aids or virgin gum - - *the earring itself!*

I break out into a cold sweat...this is the only pair of earrings I brought with me on this trip! My most beloved pair of earrings! They are the go-everywhere, matches-anything, I-got-them-on-sale-at-Loehman's-and-it-was-the-last-pair earrings!!

I jump up from my seat and begin combing the usual areas where lost earrings hide. I search my hair first, my collar, and then begin what must look to the other passengers like a very poorly executed breast exam. I then pull my blouse forward and look directly down the front, to make sure it hasn't gotten stuck somewhere. Finally, I frisk myself beginning at my hips, just in case the elusive earring has slipped down around my waistband.

No luck...the earring has left my body, which is never a good sign. At this point I awaken to my surroundings, realizing my fellow passengers are all staring at me. I blush and begin my absurd public disclaimers of "I've just lost one earring". The women frown and shake their heads side-to-side in total empathy, while the men look at me with the universal, "we don't get it" expression, "So?"

Next desperate step: I am now down on all fours in the aisle of the airplane checking not only under my own seat but the seats of passengers five rows in either direction as well. My fellow 'sisters in despair', have completely bought into my futile search. These women are even checking in their purses, as if my earring could have fallen off of my ear, leapt over three seats and landed in their bags. They are all "one earring" survivors!

This four-legged crawl continues, until I hear the pilot telling us to return to our seats for the airport approach. I call the flight attendant, explain my plight and give her my name and phone number, in the event the cleaning crew finds my earring. She is taking the information because she must; both of us know the odds of the one earring being found alive. I am now experiencing that extremely vulnerable no-earring feeling...that "I wear my hair short, I look like a boy, I feel completely naked" feeling.

I obsessed about my lost earring all weekend, which I acknowledge as unhealthy behavior. I stare at its mate and wonder to myself, "Should I just throw it away to end this torture? Should I begin a universal search for a replacement or should I just try to emotionally let it go?" I keep the earring, fully prepared to add it to my collection of earrings-with-no-mates collection that I began one month after I had my ears pierced.

I board the plane to return to Atlanta. I was not flying on my original flight so I consider the following an act of God. I take my seat and begin adjusting pillows and blankets to prepare for my nap. Suddenly, a woman three rows behind me leaps up and begins shouting, "Lady, lady, I have your earring!"

Epilogue: Am I dreaming? I look over my shoulder down the aisle to where the obviously ecstatic woman is standing. Sure enough, *she has my earring taped to a piece of cardboard with my flight number and seat assignment scratched on it!*

"When my husband and I changed clothes on Friday, I found your earring in his pants' cuff". To this day am not sure if I'm more incredulous that my earring was in random man's pant cuff or that his wife found it there. She proudly presented me with my earring, my universe returned to normal and I went to sleep - both my earrings safely tucked away in my wallet. *If you want my earring, you're going to have to take my whole purse!*

Pin Codes and Passwords

If Allen Ludden were alive today, I would recommend to him that he start a new game called "Remember Your Password!" This show would test the contestants ability to recall the dozens of mind-boggling, memory-stumping, brain-numbing access codes, number sequences and letter combinations now crucial to our high-tech existence. In addition to large piles of cash, the winner would receive an ATM card that didn't reject your request after only two misfires of your PIN (Pain in Neck!).

While this secret-squirrel approach to accessing our world is found everywhere, it has reached epidemic proportions on our computers. Each morning, I pray that, just for today, I will have the clarity of mind to get where I need to go inside this alter ego of mine. This machine has forced me to create a Windows password, a screen-saver password and a network password. All of this is before I ever even enter a program.

How foolish I was! I listened to the advice of those silly little boxes that "pop up" on your screen, theoretically to "help" you create all of the above. *"WARNING: Do not use your name, birth date or social security number as part of your password!"* That's just fine! We have just successfully eliminated the three factoids I could recall under duress. Then comes the second more ominous threat. *"For your protection, do not write your password down anywhere."*

I obey the man-in-the-box and have now successfully protected myself from myself. I don't know about you but, in my over-forty world if it isn't it writing, it is simply not happening!

Once you've passed through these barriers to entry, you are trapped in Phase II of the password game, which is create a name for yourself that hasn't already been taken. You type in your real name. It turns out to be shared by thousands, so that doesn't work! Again to "help" you, these E-mail servers and websites suggest a name for you that always includes some very bizarre set of numbers on the end. In desperation, you click OK and for the next several years you will be plagued with

5

trying to recall six digits...*that have nothing to do with anything about you!*

I have approximately a dozen or so login names for various services and accounts and all of them elude me, at one point or another. They further humiliate you, making you come up with a secret question-and-answer, just in case you forget your password. Most days I can't recall the stupid question, much less the answer!

So here's my tip to you for today. If you're married, set up your on-line bank account using your wedding anniversary date. *This will force your husband to recall how much he loved you once upon a time, each time he looks at the balance! He might even send you a card!*

Nothing is simple anymore. I long for the days when things were what they appeared to be. I spent the better part of last Thursday, trying to get duplicate keys for our new truck at the hardware store but to no avail. After four trips, I called the dealership. They finally informed me, we had an antitheft key with a computer chip, which could not be copied. I then drove to the dealership, had my $25 key made, all the while thinking to myself... *"The only people this double secret key is going to keep out of this truck is my husband and me!"*

Epilogue: I set up my Weight Watchers login using my real name and actual birth date. After all, how many people will want to break in and alter my point intake record, besides me?

Family Vacation

My family hails from Buffalo, New York. Every summer for years after we moved to Texas, we would pile ourselves in the family wagon and head north for our family vacation. The term vacation is defined as a reprieve from a routine or work. Traveling for thirty-two hours in a car with four children doesn't seem to meet that criteria but that's what our parents called it. I now refer to these sojourns as the 'Ho-Jo's Child Plate Tour of America.'

Apparently we saw all kinds of historical places along the way. While we cannot recall anything about those sites, "*The Drive*" comes back to us as though it were yesterday.

Why do all Dads think you can coordinate a car needing gas with children needing to use the rest room? I can still hear his baritone voice booming, "OK, everyone get out and use the bathroom." The refusal of this opportunity with the perfunctory response of "I don't have to go right now" meant forfeiting all future pit stop rights. So, to appease my Dad, we would all unload and go through the mandatory motions. Sixty miles later you are staring at the gas gauge, hawking the signs marking the miles to the nearest rest stop. You did not say a word until you were certain that your motion to stop would be seconded by another person in the car under the age of fifteen -- safety in numbers!

There are unwritten, unspoken rules of the road. All siblings in a car know that it is a federal offense to allow any portion of your body to spill over the designated territorial lines on the back seat. Each movement over these lines was reported immediately to a non-driving adult in the whiniest voice you could manage. "Mommmmm, Diane has her knee resting on my side of the seat and it's touching my blanket." It was irrelevant that this space was available for my sister's knee - the point was *she was in my space!* If we could not settle this argument between us, my Father's arm would miraculously extend itself from the front to the back seat (while still driving) and slap our hands. "Stretch" Armstrong had nothing on this man.

Our wagon was very chic, complete with wood paneling, a rubber luggage rack and a rumble seat. Because I was the youngest with the shortest legs, I saw over half of America backwards. The only time I could ride in the front was the graveyard shift, when my ability to chatter non-stop kept Dad awake. I don't recall this being exactly "quality time".

We have at least fifty carousels of slides my Father took of our motley crew, as evidence that we did see Williamsburg, Arlington Cemetery, the Empire State Building, etc... Each slide managed to capture us in all of our splendor. Mom, is there any particular reason why I was wearing green plaid peddle-pushers with a brown striped top? She defends our wardrobe selection with tales of suitcases at the bottom of the stack, spilled drinks on the matching top and general hysteria.

Sometimes my Mother would take a picture of the rest of us. You can distinguish her photos by either the thumb shadow in the upper right corner or the fact that no one's head appears in the frame. These pictures probably depict the actual mood better than my father's slide photos!

Epilogue: I was watching several families at the airport last weekend, wondering if family vacations on a plane have their own set of miserable moments. No pit stops, no car bingo, no Howard Johnson's child's plate, no flat tires, no Dairy Queen? We boarded the plane and I was closing my eyes to sleep when I heard the faint, whiny voice of a child in front of me, "Mom, when are gonna get there?" O.K., so maybe it is the same.

Jiggidy Jig

"Home again, home again Jiggidy Jig," I chanted aloud as I do each and every time I return home from anywhere. My sister Marsha was with me and she begins to laugh hysterically. "Why are you laughing?" I asked her wondering what could be so funny about pulling into a driveway. "Do you know why you say Jiggidy -Jig?" I ponder her question. It's not like nursery rhymes are a part of my everyday reality.

It's a Mom thing. This is yet another habit, which has passed from generation to generation completely unbeknownst to we, her children. Why was my sister laughing at me? Because, she too, recites 'Jiggidy Jig' each time she returns home. Her sons, Paul and Mark, apparently place bets as to exactly when this little rhyme will fall from her lips. Not if mind you, when!

It appears that only two of the four children in our family inherited the little pig gene. How fortunate for Marsha and me. I confirmed this last week when I saw my nephew David. "Does your Mother say "Jiggidy Jig" when she pulls the car into your driveway?" His blank stare was all the answer I needed. I should probably go back and explain that question to him one day. My brother's children weren't present but something tells me that he too has been spared.

Although Marsha and I have an exclusive on this particular trait, there is so much more we all four share. For instance, we all got the "shopping bag exchange" gene. This is to say that, wherever two or more of us are gathered, we are trading stuff. Borrowed stuff...new stuff...a third party's stuff...doesn't matter. What matters is that you come in with your bag and you leave with another one. I'm in this loop and I live 800 miles away from them, explain that!

We are very practical about the exchange. You would think there would be events and locations where this would be considered inappropriate, such as church. Nope, there are no boundaries in this game. Your only goal is to grab the right bag and hope that you've traded up. Plastic grocery bags are for amateur traders. Paper sacks with no handles are strictly forbidden. If you want to trade in our family, you have to have a shopping bag with handles!

We have mastered the subtleties of "the exchange", such that non-family onlookers never even know this is going on before their very eyes. When you enter a room, you place your bag in a corner or behind a piece of furniture and you make eye contact with the recipient of the bag. You simply nod or mouth the words, "Here's your stuff", and then begin your greetings. No need to talk about what's in the bag, this has all been pre-arranged.

If no family gathering is imminent and you need your items returned, then we punt and use either the drop-off or passing techniques. This is where you call sibling/child A who you will be seeing, who will be visiting sibling/child C, who you will not be seeing, but who you have a bag for. If this can't be managed, you simply drop it off at the back door and leave a voice mail.

Epilogue: It is important to stay close to your family. It makes you feel less weird. I depend on my Mother's idiosyncrasies, like I depend on the sun rising. While Paul and Mark might not admit it today, they will one day find comfort in their Mother's silly, but predictable behavior... *"Home again, home again, Jiggidy Jig!"*

Define Emergency

"Sharon, you can use the gas credit card, but only in an emergency", stated my fiscally conservative Father, circa 1980. **Emergency, n: A sudden or unexpected occurrence demanding prompt action.** How vague is that!

OK, so my definition of emergency varied ever so slightly from that of my dad's. The gap on these already nebulous instructions widened when the gas station located one mile from my apartment during college started selling chips, cigarettes and beer.

Let's see, it is Saturday night, we have no money and we want to play. Refer back to the above definition. Well duh, of course that's an emergency. Let's all run get $5.00 worth of gas and charge $20.00 worth of emergency supplies.

What in the Sam hill did I think my Father was going to say when my gas bill increased by 100% during one fall semester? Can you imagine? There was actually a small part of me that thought, he either; a) Wouldn't notice or, b) Wouldn't care? My father is an Engineer who holds an undergraduate degree in math - - HE NOTICED! He was raised during the Depression - - HE CARED!

The most delusional train of thought one experiences during adolescence is the belief that you can outsmart your parents. This was not only inaccurate but proved to be a very bad strategic error. Oh my gosh, it makes me cringe just thinking about it! While I have blocked out most of the memory to save myself from complete shame, I do recall weaving tales of roadside emergencies, running out of gas and unplanned (but very necessary) trips. Exactly how do parents keep from laughing in their children's faces the ten minutes just before they ground them for the rest of their lives?

When I went to school, we survived on about $250 a month. This covered all non-tuition expenses, including rent. The disposable income in this monthly budget reflects what is now one trip to Walmart! We survived these rather strict budgetary confinements and still managed to have a very good time through communal living - - we pooled our limited resources. If 50 very poor collegiate students all chip in two dollars, a *good time* can be had.

My father might have been more prepared for my shenanigans if only one of my three older siblings had an ounce of irreverence in them. I love them dearly, but couldn't they have gotten in a little trouble to make life easier for me? *Did they all have to make a 4.0 and never use the gas card?*

Fortunately for me, even if I still had the same whims of a young, somewhat wild, college student, my body would no longer "go there". I had to pull an "all-nighter" one year ago to prepare for an event and I was dysfunctional for five days afterwards!

Epilogue: I learned a very important lesson only three years after my gas card escapades. I took a sabbatical and then went back to school to complete my degree. I went back on my dime. My father had learned some lessons also and I was not equipped with his gas card on this round. Never use the word *"emergency"* with your child without first defining the terms.

It's Fun to Dress at the Y-M-C-A!?

Not only was I going to work out at the gym, I was going to attempt to successfully shower and change clothes in the locker room! I was so proud of myself for trying as I have failed at this mission before.

There is a species of females in the locker room I am unfamiliar with. They are the "quick change artists". These women can walk in the locker room, perspiring heavily from their high impact aerobic class and walk out a mere thirty minutes later in a business suit and hose. I've been observing these women for years, wondering what class in womanhood they took that I somehow missed. There is no other explanation as there are able to stand in a room with 150% humidity---and still get their hair to dry perfectly. As if this alone wouldn't make you hate them, they then pull off perfect makeup, under lighting that rivals an operating room.

You must have the exact right bag of tricks to pull off changing away from "home base". A bag of tricks I have been trying to assemble for years now. Just once, I want to walk out of that locker room in a pretty, white silk blouse and the right color lingerie underneath it.

Take tonight for instance. I had tennis at 6:00 PM and a meeting at church at 7:15. My window was 30 minutes. I was determined to make it work. Let's start with the first issue, which is "The Towel". You can't jam a big enough towel into your nifty little work out bag, so you have to use something that looks like an oversized washcloth. Since you can't fit a beach towel in there, you sure can't fit a robe. So you end up dashing from the shower to the changing room pretty much half-naked. Some women stroll, I run.

I dried off with this washcloth equivalent and put my clothes on. So far, so good. I move on to the hair and makeup phase. It is not easy to take hair from dripping wet to neatly coifed in what is now 17 minutes left on the clock. Make that impossible. I combed in some mousse and decided I would roll down all the car windows on the way to the meeting. Not a trick you should try, when the outcome really matters.

The makeup portion of this drill is usually the only area that I get a gold star. I'm organized---I carry my whole face in one little pouch, so I wasn't worried. Not tonight. Tonight my foundation is in my purse! *My purse is in my car!* I give up. I can't do it. I can't be one of "them". Two minutes left. I glance over at one of the "quick change artists", touching up her lipstick. At this point I'm saying to myself, "She's probably a shallow person, I hope she's a shallow person! Surely she is a completely shallow person." Petty; a place I go some days out of self-defense!

Epilogue: I'm late, I'm running to the car. I throw my stuff in the back seat, start the engine and pull out of my parking spot. I **hear a grating noise! Something is loose beneath my car!** I stop the car, the noise stops. I back up some more and it begins again.

I hardly noticed the woman waving her arms at me from the tennis courts. I could see her mouth moving, but couldn't make out what she was saying. I lean out the window as she comes closer. "Lady, you've got a hair dryer hanging out of your car?" *Of course I do!!* I get out, put the thing inside my car and leave this forsaken place. *Does anyone know where the make-up classes for how-to-be-a-together woman are held?*

Driving Miss Abby

Why we made such a big to-do over high paid athletes when we have super stars walking amongst us? *Everyone with a two-year-old, come get your trophy!!* "Driving Miss Abby" is the title for the weekend spent with my dear friend, Ruth, and her daughter, Abigail, visiting me. Abby has two gears, high and off. You can entertain, distract and discipline. The net result is the same -- constant motion. My personal favorite is when you have the two-year-old child snuggled in your lap and you think you are reading them to sleep. You are enjoying the quaint little story when *...suddenly*, you lose their attention completely. They stiffen and straighten out their little body, starting to slide down toward the floor. To escape is their goal, to simply touch those little feet to the floor and become mobile again. It's like wresting an animated two-by-four.

In Abigail's case, driving is the only activity that lulls this precious child to sleep. At some point on Friday night I had fallen asleep on the couch. I was awakened around 12:30 AM by the jingling of keys at the door. Ruth was leaving the house in her robe, with a very awake Abigail in tow. In an effort to be a good friend and congenial hostess, I drug myself off the couch and volunteered to go with them. Thirty minutes later, I was sound asleep in the front seat and Abigail was pointing at all the trucks, with her eyes as big as saucers.

We all did finally sleep. I woke up at six the next morning and did what I should have done before they arrived. I took everything within two-year-old reach, shoved it in a box and hid it in my closet. In my naiveté, I thought that you only had to remove items with curb-appeal, such as brightly colored objects, things that glittered, talked or moved. I realized how wrong I was when I looked over and saw Abby slinging a fifth of Scotch across my living room that she had confiscated from the bar. Funny, she didn't want to open the bottle. She just wanted to carry it to where I was. "Thank you, Abby", I said, promptly hiding it.

Now let's talk a minute about the whole car seat thing. I am reporting that, if I had a two-year-old, I would *never* leave my home. I don't care how handy these pop-up, fold-up, hold-'em-in-tight devices are, they are still high maintenance. So, when I tell you that "we" went shopping on Saturday, what I really mean is, I drove the getaway car. This is apparently a Mother's total fantasy. To be able to run into a store, buy what you need and come back, without having to remove your child from the car seat.

Managing the "gear" is a job in-and-of itself. When we were packing them up to leave on Sunday, I was in charge of disassembling the travel bed. No problem, I'd seen Ruth do it in about two seconds. That bed would *still* be in my room or we would have moved it in an upright position, if 'Mom' had not been around!

Epilogue: I have always respected Ruth, but now I salute her. I salute my Mom and every other mom who has loved a child through this age of wonder. I know I'm too old for this, since I can't even remember where I ended up hiding the Scotch. Give these women a trophy!

My VCR Taunts Me Still

My VCR taunts me still. I can send thousands of database names over the Internet, talk to someone in Africa on-line, yet I still can't record a movie while I'm out of the house (or in the house, for that matter)! Record one movie while watching another show!?! Don't even think about it. Bootleg a movie using two VCR's!?! Only in my dreams!

I have studied under a master, my Mother's husband, Jay. Jay has been "not recording" movies for years. To my mother's knowledge, they have never captured an entire film on a tape. In Jay's most recent attempt to record "Hello Dolly", my mother turned on the TV and switched channels. The end product: four continuous hours of The Weather Channel!!

Apparently there is always a break down in communication, which is somewhat surprising as it's just the two of them living in that house. Jay toils away setting up the VCR to record while he's at work. The housekeeper comes and, while dusting, changes the speed setting. This little slip of the dust buster yields the most common VCR mishap - - a movie with no ending - - the ultimate tease. Jay has true grit. He still believes that one day he will have the classic movie collection of his dreams.

Not me. Like many others, I had an incident that caused me to abandon recording movies and move on to the next level of technology, without ever graduating from the last level. I quit VCR three years ago, when I attempted to record the first of three nights of a mini-series. I got home, put on my pajamas and settled on the couch all jazzed to watch my movie. I hit play and after five minutes of denial I had to admit to myself that I had inadvertently captured Monday Night Football. Of all things! I fast-forwarded through the whole tape thinking that maybe, just maybe there had been a Presidential address and my show was delayed. Nope, I missed the whole thing. I extinguished my candles and my last ray of hope and threw the tape away. I haven't tried to record since that fateful night.

Clearly, the play-only VCR would have worked for me, but like many folks, I was seduced by all the nifty features. I am part of a growing group of S.T.U.'s (Surface Technology Users). Who are we? We are the people who purchase the latest gizmo in hopes of remaining on the cutting edge and then under-utilize it completely. I will come completely clean - I never have even programmed my phones for speed dialing (circa 1980). "Mom, what's Jeff's (her son, my brother) work number?" " I don't know". "Don't you ever call him at work?" "Yes, but the number is programmed in the phone and I don't have it written down anywhere". "So, let me get this straight...unless you are standing in your master bedroom at that particular phone, you cannot call your own son at work? Does that sound like progress to you?"

My new cell phone could probably drive my car for me, if I could just program the thing. Who in the world has time to read those instruction guides? Plus, they change the game just to keep you on your toes. The number two used to be the universal SAVE message button. Now it's three, or seven or whatever. The truth? We are all leaving each other messages that are never heard because the cell phone industry can't just pick a number!

EPilogue: Before you technology gurus turn you nose up at me or any other technology-challenged individual know this: we, the S.T.U.'s, do not hold back technology advancement - - we underwrite it.

Vanity vs. Sanity

The principal difference between youth and adulthood is this - - we, the adults, are willing to sacrifice appearance for functionality. Take today, for instance. Hugh and I are going with some friends to float down a river. Twenty-plus years ago, I would have done my hair and make-up, put on a new bathing suit and a cute pair of white tennis shoes. This non-functional-but-cute outfit would have lasted for the first five minutes of the expedition. Upon entering the river itself, it would have all been in vain. Today I am equipped with, 1) A bathing suit I don't mind tearing on a random rock and, 2) A pair of shorts I could [would?], if necessary, sacrifice completely. The white tennis shoes that would have looked spiffy up to the point they got wet and muddy, have been traded for a pair of very ugly, but lightweight and sturdy, water shoes. These are quite possibly the worse looking things I've ever put on my feet.

I would have worn jewelry that matched my ensemble - - today I have on none. Most notably, I will be sporting an old t-shirt to protect my shoulders from the sun, representing the ultimate forfeiture of vanity-for-sanity. If the twenty-year-old me was here today she would not get in the car with me, much less the same boat. The twenty-year-old me would also be crying most of the way home, because she had lost one of her favorite earrings, ruined her best bathing suit and cut her knee, when she slipped and fell in those cute little (no longer white!) tennis shoes.

There are other advantages of having an adult perspective. My new employer equips their reps with a mini-van. Having never been a mom or a suburban home owner until recently, I can tell you that this would **not** have been my first choice for a car. Like millions of others, I was the proud owner of a S.U.V., which even young people proclaim to be "cool". It took only twenty minutes for me to fall in love with this van and I could now care less if it appears as though I am driving carpool everywhere I go. My sister-in-law, Camille, said it perfectly. "Driving around in a mini-van is like driving around in a huge purse." She is so right! You can take everything you own with you, accessing anything inside with ease using one of the six doors. I adore my new "purse". I don't care if it's not the fastest or sportiest on the road. I have finally found a vehicle that works for me *and* my back. No youth-approved "cool" car could seduce me away from the "purse."

The real telling "adulthood" moment happened a week ago. Hugh came inside after mowing the lawn. He was sweaty and grimy, heading straight for our new living room furniture. "Wait", I heard myself yell to him. I ran to the linen closet, returning with the big Kahuna of "looks ridiculous now, but makes you thankful later" items: a sheet to cover the couch. Wow, I *am* my Mother.

Epilogue: Young people possess the priceless gift of living in the moment. There is much to be learned from them on this front. When you are young, consequences are inconsequential. Let's admit to ourselves what we can't tell our youth. What we call foresight is really only hindsight, *twenty years after the fact*. My lifelong challenge is this: how can I live in the present and still not ruin "my cute little tennis shoes?"

The White House Ball

At 8:40 AM this morning I left the house for a 10:00 AM flight and I still had to drop my dog Champ off at the kennel. I am breaking all land speed records -- *I cannot miss this flight.* You see, due to some rare good fortune, I was attending the White House Christmas Ball with some friends.

I landed the car safely at the park 'n ride place. I haul my bags out and run up to the bag-checking place, where you take the weary traveler pledge: Yes, yes, yes -- these bags have been with me the whole time! Yes, yes, yes -- I packed them myself! No, I haven't accepted any packages from a stranger. I have wondered for some time why they believe a person with mal intent would say NO to these questions but that's another issue. Anyway, we finish the whole process, the man looks at me and says the dreaded words ------ "Sorry lady, your flight has been canceled."

"Excuse me! What did you say??", I ask, standing two inches from this poor man's face. "You'll have to step inside to the ticket counter and see what they can do." Man number two -- "Sorry lady, (they're all sorry) there's not a flight I can confirm you on today. You can fly standby for all of our afternoon flights." The meltdown begins. "Look, this isn't some business meeting I can miss (priorities!). This is a once-in-a-lifetime invitation to the White House Christmas party, *you have to get me on a plane."* This man clearly had not taken customer sensitivity training since he replied glibly with, "If it was me and I had something that important to go to, I would have left yesterday".

The following six hours at the airport were not pretty and by that point, I could have just as easily ridden my broom to the event. I did board another flight, but it was canceled due to mechanical problems. I did finally make the cut for a plane that was actually departing but not without incident. The flight attendant tried to tell me that I couldn't bring my carry-on on the plane. She was attempting to help me by grabbing the handle and I have a death grip on the thing saying, "You don't understand what will happen if this gown and I do not make it to D.C. by 5:00 PM today! Sorry lady but me and this bag are traveling together."

The story has a happy ending. By 8:00 o'clock, I was standing in front of the White House with my friends. This is the one night they let people take pictures, so I am running around like the ingénue that I am snapping, clicking, and flashing away. I got some fabulous pictures, pictures I could never replace. I even took once-in-a-lifetime photos for other people...Congressmen included! They were too proud to bring their own camera, but very grateful someone had one.

I was completely out of my element, didn't know the name or face of a soul there, besides my friends and the President and First Lady (I suffer no delusions of grandeur - I was invisible). I tried to have polite conversation with some people, but mostly, I just took pictures.

Epilogue: Two days later, I am standing in front of the capitol for the lighting of the Christmas tree. I am getting some more great shots and yet I had this nagging thought of "Gosh, this roll of film is taking an extraordinary number of pictures." My friend grabs the camera and breaks the news, "Sharon, there is no film in your camera." And so ends the story of *Ms. Thing goes to Washington.* NO pictures, NO proof!!! Not even a lousy T-shirt.

Road Roof Kill

It was very sultry and moonless night in 1977 when me and my high school soul sisters; Allison, Lisa and Nancy, happened upon the scattered contents of a woman's purse. We were walking close to my house where we first found her wallet. About twenty feet away, we spotted her checkbook. After another thirty feet, we found her essentials such as hair spray, makeup bag, etc....

Because we were young drama-queens-in-training, we concocted a theory. The purse owner had been abducted; she had been running from her pursuer, and had dropped her purse in the chase!! We panicked...we called the police...we spent the next four hours enveloped in a mini-series of our own making!

At close to midnight that same evening, we learned the terrible truth. The woman had driven away from a club three miles away, with her purse on the roof of her car. The purse had hung on for dear life for two-and-a-half miles until it just gave up and fell off on a tricky curve near my house. The police finally located the woman, to tell her that three girls (how dare he call us girls!) had recovered her purse and all of its contents. These stories rarely have such happy endings...I mean... how often does Nancy Drew & Co. find and return a "stolen" purse?

I flashbacked to the flying purse incident when my friend, Rebecca, called me terribly upset from her car phone. She had just witnessed her new sunglasses fly off the back of her car. Not dime store sunglasses; but the ninety-dollar variety that you feel guilty about buying. When she called me she was on the highway going sixty miles per hour and was seriously considering backing up to get her glasses! I would too! I have sacrificed at least fifty soft drinks, one day-timer and one purse to *"Car Roof Road Kill"!*

So Rebecca is about to return for her sunglasses yet we drive around all day seeing HUGE items abandoned on the highways. How many of us have almost met our maker because there is a mattress or chair in our lane? Did the drivers just not notice a one hundred pound, ten square foot, item leaving the roof of their car?

I suppose it's all the same. I did not know my purse had received a traffic burial, until I got home and went to grab my checkbook. I played back my departure from the mall parking lot only to realize that this was when I had last seen my purse alive! You grieve your personal items differently, when you lose them in this manner. You don't feel violated or angry - - you feel stupid and frustrated. This frustration lives anew each time you go to find something which was, of course, in your purse or your day-timer. "Where is that $45 store credit from Marshall's?" you wonder to yourself. "Oh yeh, I stuck it in my purse! " You bow your head for a moment of silence for your old pal, your purse; so difficult to accept that its end was met in such a tragic and useless way.

Epilogue: Later that night, Rebecca called me, laughing hysterically. She had just gotten home from her four year old's birthday party, at Chucky Cheese. She was pulling out from the parking lot and happened to glance in her rear view mirror. Out of the corner of her eye, she saw behind her an open box of pizza, lying in the middle of the road. "No way", she thinks to herself..."**That couldn't be our pizza? I couldn't have two car roof casualties in one day?**"

She gets home to confirm the sad truth. Her husband, George, had indeed put the pizza on her car while he was putting the baby in. Thought for sure she would see it there before she pulled away. *Whoops!*

24

All's Fair?

I am trying so hard not to sweat the small stuff it is giving me a case of the hives. Intellectually I realize that there are things that I am just supposed to let go of. I know this logically, yet still, some of life's most inconsequential goings-on fly in the face of how I was raised.

I hail from a family of six, two big sisters and one big brother, all born two years apart. We were the quintessential Middle America family growing up. No, we were not the Cleavers. Actually, we were as dazed and confused as the next family, but no one spoke of those things then. The outward and visible hallmarks of being part of Middle America in the 50's and 60's were as follows: We drank Kool–Aid, not soft drinks; we took family vacations in a station wagon, not a plane; we made cookies from scratch, no "store bought" cookies; and our mother sewed most of our dresses.

Another, then annoying, trademark of that era was that virtues and values were taught through everyday tasks. Mom taught us about being fair at an early age through desert portions. If one of us was put in charge of making pudding, jell-o or just serving up ice cream, the person dishing it up was the last to pick their serving. Great effort was taken to make sure the portions were evenly distributed, as the slightest variation meant you would lose out on a mouthful of whatever. This same rule applied to the pie served every Sunday, as a special treat. You might remember these frozen delicacies, as they had little whip cream humps around the edge. Slicing the pie down the middle wasn't good enough for our family; we counted the total number of humps and divided by six. Apparently there was never an even amount of humps and so each of us got 6.5 humps per person. They threw a little math in there as well!

Other fairness issues were taught simply by being one of four children in a home with only one children's bathroom. You had to get in and out of there fast, with the only exception being prom night or soaking an injury. Repercussions for not obeying this unwritten law ranged from sibling warfare to parental intervention. Neither option was pretty. We also applied the "what's fair" rule to hogging the television, who got to sit in the front seat and the amount of your allowance. There was a direct correlation between chores and allowance that I'm pretty sure is the basis of our work ethics.

It is no small wonder I entered adulthood thinking everyone played by these same "fair" rules. I believed people asked themselves if what they were doing was fair, before doing it. Why? I thought that they, like me, thought justice for all meant justice for themselves as well. I can barely get over it when I'm standing in a long checkout line, they suddenly open a new line and the last person in my line goes to the front of the new line. *I know* you know what I mean!

Epilogue: Am I foolish enough to believe that all in life is fair? No, I just think, **whomever "is counting the humps and cutting the pie" should pick last**, that's all. Apply this rule to a few of your favorite equality issues and let me know what you think.

911 Tribute

September 15, 2001

W e cling to the familiar. We move in what feels like robotic motion. We are still unable to grasp what it means to have our nation and our fellow citizens attacked! We go through daily routines and rote tasks, trying to keep it together, lest we fall apart. We view pictures on the television that still seem surreal. Photographs that seem ripped from a sensational movie but this was not a movie

I have not wept yet and I know my tears will be misplaced, when they do come. I will cry one day, when my car won't start...or when the ice tray gets jammed. Like millions of Americans, I will weep from a frustration so profound, it yields to anger, gives way to rage. I fear my rage. Because I know it can consume me. Rage, I've learned, is the only enemy that can defeat my spirit. I have asked myself a million times...*What kind of righteous rage fueled these attacks on our fellow Americans?*

I find myself infuriated that we must move forward, because it does not seem fair. I watch the citizens of New York and I am compelled to be there with them...to do something that matters...something that counts...something to help! I have sat paralyzed listening to and watching the reports feeling that if I left, I would be somehow abandoning these victims.

We pay our respects silently and prayerfully. And from the rubble and the ashes, there grows a respect for humankind...a profound sense of unity...a new understanding of what freedom really is...a freedom which has been attacked in a most profound way. We search our souls, but there is no place in our minds or our hearts to put an event this tragic, this useless, and this devastating

We salute the volunteers, the fire fighters, the police force, and our Nation's leaders. We die inside for the friends and families of the victims, whose courage and whose grief are beyond our comprehension. They have dug deep to bring forth the best of who they are and they are patriots all.

Our lives will never be the same. Suddenly, our Nation, operating as individuals, is woven together by our humanity. Our differences have melted in the flames and we have become one. Each of us listens to the heartbreaking stories told by friends who had a friend, who had a loved one, in the twin towers or at the Pentagon. I sit miles and miles away, somehow knowing the Americans who are directly and personally touched by this horrific travesty, who will grieve forever!

Epilogue: One seven-year-old child in New York, asked what he wished for said..."I wish we could go back and make it not happen."

Because it is not within anyone's power to grant this young boy his wish, we move forward together. We can honor the heroes' lives through our faith...our lives...our spirit...our resilience. *We have said it before, but perhaps none of us fully understood the power and the plea behind those words, "**God Bless America!**"*

This Sign's for You

We were on the last half-mile portion of the three-mile walk, "We" being my friend, Roy, and I. Roy is my closest male friend and a trusted advisor. We walk this walk often. Over the years we have fallen into quite a routine. By routine, I do not mean the pace of our walk, although we do have a set speed. I am referring to the "**Problem Time Sharing**" routine we have unwittingly devised. Our "time share" system has never been discussed so, it might come as a surprise to Roy that it even exists!

Our three-mile walk is one giant loop. Not a track, not a circle, not a straightaway...a loop. The unspoken rule is, whoever spills their guts on the way up, has to listen to the other person's "stuff" on the way back. It's a very civil arrangement. No one ever looks at their watch and says, "Your time is up, it's my turn to talk now". It is understood, in the way it only can be between old friends. You've got old friends--you understand what I mean.

Unless there is a crisis or another important matter requiring extra attention, you instinctively share the floor. Filibustering was devised to kill bills...*It can do the same thing to a conversation!* So, while listening is a good thing, let's face it, we all want to get *Our* story out there. Since our entire ego rests on validation, it is no small wonder why we all want and need to be heard.

Another unspoken rule is, you cannot pull out a zinger in the last segment of the walk. But on this particular day, when near the end...Roy tells me the reason he isn't doing anything about the situation he had just explained was, he was "waiting for a Sign". A "Sign"? A "Sign"...what in the world do you mean by that?"

I am a woman of impulse and action. I've not so much waited for a pause in activity, much less a sign. So I can barely wrap my mind around this concept. I always thought "Signs" was just the name of the song from the psychedelic '60's.

His explanation was fascinating. *The "Sign" did not have to have anything to do with the subject matter!* It could be a good sign...or a bad sign. The sign could be dramatic or subtle; it didn't matter. The bottom line was..."the Sign" could basically be any event happening to or around him that deviated from his normal routine.

So, here we are, on "Sign-Watch-Day-Ten". It is making me nuts. I want action taken, for better or for worse. We were at dinner last night and I'm wondering, if the waiter spills that hot coffee on you, is that a "Sign"? If one of those baseball guys get another home run tonight, is that a "Sign"? *Send this man a "SIGN"...before I lose my mind!!*

Epilogue: Listening is an art; a lost art in many ways. I don't want to leave you with the impression either Roy or I simply wait for the "turn in the road". We listen and share. We both feel a little more understood and a lot more hopeful, about life in general. I'm now thinking...maybe this story, being published for many to read, will do the trick. **Roy, this sign is for you!**

Phase One of a Relationship

I am in a Phase One relationship right now. If pressed, I could probably recite chapter and verse of the dialogue between Ed and me since our First Encounter. Whether you are married or single, I'm sure you have very vivid memories of a relationship in Phase One, when *everything matters*. *Every* word uttered...*Every* inflection used...*Every* voice mail... *Every* kiss...*Every* hand holding...*Every* door-opening detail.

Suffice to say, things are moving forward. I have held myself in check for three months and not discussed the relationship with Ed. I have enough male friends to know the four most dreaded words as defined by the male race are, "We need to talk!" This can never mean anything good for a male. They know that...We know that.

We frankly might as well say---"I'd like to lessen the chances of whatever this is surviving by 99% by discussing something with you that my girlfriends and I have been obsessing over and which will come as a complete shock to you! And, after we're done discussing this relationship, I'll go home and feel hopeful and serene while you can go home and take my number off your autodial!"

Another common compulsion in Phase One relationships is to try and put only your best foot forward. Yes, I admit it, I have been trying to impress Ed with my wit...my charm ...my compassion and, of course...my total love of exercise and fitness (O.K., so the latter is a *slight* exaggeration of the truth).

Suffice to say, this ego-driven charade came back to roost last weekend, when I was telling Ed that I now swim laps every morning. In order for the full impact of this situation to be felt, you must understand how we look after using a treadmill pales in comparison to the sight of a woman in, A) A bathing suit, with no semblance of a tan, B) Swim goggles vintage Amelia Earhart and, C) A bathing cap, which, although it has no plastic flowers, might as well have. Imagine my panic when, after my subtle mentioning of my workout that morning, Ed pipes up with, " Next time I come and see you, I am going to bring my bathing suit, so that we can swim laps together!"

My immediate but unspoken reaction is, of course, *"I don't think so!!* In fact, I feel a six month cold coming on". Thirty seconds pass after Ed's innocent seed has been planted. I have still not recovered enough to come back with, "Gosh, you know that sounds great, but men and women over twelve can't swim together at my club - pool rules. I think all the clubs in the Bible Belt have that rule".

The most fascinating thing about this is Ed's complete inability to comprehend that swimming laps is not something I'd like to do together...for what I consider to be fairly obvious reasons. I have spent three months putting together my most flattering ensembles. Am I going to destroy that all for a lap in the pool? *After we swim, why don't we go and stand under some bathroom lights for a while...and then tell each other how much we weigh?*

I realize that solid relationships are built on openness and trust. But...can't we save some of this for Phase Two or Three?

Epilogue: A week has passed since this swim-together comment. This thing is hanging out there like a time bomb for me. Needless to say, I have not mentioned swimming since then. In fact, I hesitate to order water with dinner for fear it might remind him of the pool! *I will let you know IF we make it to Phase Two!*

Advice is Not Cheap!

Whoever coined the phrase advice is cheap...*never* paid my long distance bill! I have been known to place calls regaling my friends with my "question du jour", until I hit a person with the *"right"* answer. *The right answer is simply that response which validates what I was going to do anyway!!* By the by, I'm not talking about legal, financial or business advice. I will be the first to admit, I should always seek help in these matters. I am now speaking of relationship advice. Those moments when your brain is only involved as a mechanism to process what your gut, your heart wants you to do.

When I am faced with a tough decision, I call upon my oldest and dearest friend, Kathy. Kathy has represented the opposing viewpoint for me for thirty-five years. Suffice to say, if I can "sell" her, I can move forward with total peace of mind.

I usually call late, after I've had an entire evening to build my case. After our normal pleasantries, the dialogue usually goes something like this..."So, do you think I should call him?" Funny, I ask this question knowing I might as well be querying if pigs can fly. I then launch into my top ten reasons why the call should be placed...to this man who is ignoring me. Kathy responds with her litany..."Maybe he's just not calling because he's busy. Maybe he doesn't want to seem too interested. Or maybe (dialogue recommended exclusively for *only best* friends), he's not interested in seeing you again. Doesn't matter why, you can't call him."

After this brutal presentation of the reality Kathy will usually soften up and ask me questions that I already know the answer to, such as "Do you really want to pursue a man who is that aloof? or..."don't you want to be with someone who really cares about you?" Sometimes, only sometimes, something she says rings true. Some bit of information sneaks past my wall of defiance and I begin to listen. Or better said, my heart begins to listen, so I can then alter my course of action.

It is very rare when I offer up unsolicited advice to my friends...*because I've realized they're not buying what I'm selling, either!* The most prevalent advice seeking is done to bridge the gender gap...and even those discussions normally go unheeded. "No, Will, I wouldn't talk to Leslie about having your wedding reception at the office. I mean, women are funny about these things, they don't want to feel like they are clipping coupons for their wedding!"

Sometimes you think you have someone sold on your advice, when you really haven't even made a dent in his or her thinking. They nod their head in agreement, they say things like, "Yeah, you're right, I won't say anything." They then leave your presence and summarily dismiss the entire conversation. If you are close friends, you run the risk of having the dreaded checkup conversation days, sometimes weeks later. "Hey, you didn't ever share that absurd idea with Leslie, did you?" Silence...followed by a very meek, "Let's just say I'm not going to go there again".

Epilogue: A friend of mine once wrote... *"I have never, under any circumstances, been able to change how I feel, by changing what I think"!* I agree--nuff said.

Rebate Man!

I recently spent approximately seven hours to study, purchase and handle the paperwork for a thirteen-dollar rebate! How's that for a sound use of time? I work on commission, so for me the expression, "time is money", is very real. I can usually take a look at a particular project and, in some form or fashion, compute an hourly rate. Sometimes I win, sometimes I lose. That's the calculated risk I take. It has taken me years to eliminate work habits and personal compulsions that are just giant consumers of time, with no payoff either personally or financially. My personal favorite time-waster for years was methodically alphabetizing random business cards that I never so much as looked at ever once they had been filed.

However, there is no sale, no store brand, no coupon in the world that can suck me in like a mail-in rebate. While I am an overt spendthrift, there lives deep inside me a miser who shops rebates for the love of the game. It is a game of discipline. The rebate world is so complicated, so detailed and so convoluted, that I am drawn to the madness of it all. Not only do you have to make sure you are buying the right size of the right brand. You have to save your receipt, save the rebate form, fill out the rebate form and mail it all in with a self-addressed, self-stamped envelope. Furthermore, all of these hoops must be jumped through before the receipt turns back into just a piece of paper…when the clock strikes midnight on a particular date.

Let's acknowledge, before we go any further, greater than half of these rebate forms are never looked at again after we leave the store. They become part of that pile in your kitchen that is home to such items as: warranty forms belonging to ten-dollar clocks (has anyone ever mailed one of those in???), pizza coupons that expired last year and sauce packets from last month's Chinese take-out..

But, if you do follow-through, don't dare try to fool the rebate gods by mailing it in a day or two late, because they live for that stuff. I now believe that there is one little man who handles all the rebates in the world that are actually paid. This gnome-like man is handling all of our forms, whether it is for a computer or canned vegetables. He sits at a table, surrounded by piles and piles of mail, tossing them out for one reason or another. He smiles to himself as he narrows the winners down to ten. He begrudgingly admits defeat on these ten, takes out his Genera-check book and issues us our checks. Then he takes all of our self-addressed envelopes with our stamps, cuts them out and resells them in the black market for a quarter! *Rebate Man is a multi-millionaire!*

Epilogue: Money has no real value, except that it can sometimes buy us time. And rebates take time to get us not very much money back. And then there is that whole question of the time-value of money. "They" told me to expect my check within ninety days; if I didn't hear back to call a 1-800 number. *I doubt Rebate Man can answer all those calls.*

Father Knows Best

*H*ow is it that I am thirty-eight years old and am afraid to call my Father about a trip I am taking? I will be gone for two weeks. I contemplated calling him right before I leave, never mentioning the trip and then just playing the odds he won't call while I'm gone. I am going to Africa in a month. I have the sore arms to prove it. There I was, in the Doctor's office, spellbound as he reeled off shots for the various names of rare diseases I could catch. Being the paranoid that I am, I kept agreeing to the next round. " Sure, sign me up," said the naive woman, who thought shots were $10 a-piece. As it turns out, I was only off by about $60 per unnecessary shot.

Anyway, I love my Dad and he loves me. But we do not see exactly eye to eye on how one invests their resources of time and money. This gap is broadened when you factor in the whole potential danger thing. I speak from experience on this issue. After college, I joined the Peace Corps and lived in Paraguay, South America. During that time, the war over the Falkland Islands broke out between Britain and Argentina. My Dad did not think that 1,000 miles was far enough away to be safe and launched a campaign to get me to come home. I won't bore you with details, except to say that the U.S. State Department was involved!

Fathers, as a rule, do not endorse the whole adventure concept for their daughters. Adventure to my Dad is Six Flags at night. They must accept that we are adults now, captains of our own destiny, women of independent means!

The problem is, my case on independence is not very strong, as I was a financial late bloomer. I am still in trouble for not keeping mileage and repair records on my first car in the nifty little auto record book my dad made for me. I admit, I didn't do much for that first car in terms of T.L.C. – adding oil to the engine was an optional item. *Changing the oil* was a total luxury! The car died in 1992 of dehydration - - all because I didn't keep the book.

I have been practicing how I am going to explain to Dad, a group of five of us going to a place with some political unrest, to bring medical supplies to a group of children who have lost their parents to AIDS. My Dad will hear the following -- **Unrest** and **AIDS**. It is my guess, our discussion will not progress much past this point.

For all my need to be on my own, I wish he lived close by. I want him to hang pictures properly, negotiate repair work being done and assure me a man is stupid when he/they don't love me anymore! That's what Dads are for -- it's their job.

Epilogue: Here's the good news! My Father, like millions of other parental units, does not believe in, and therefore does not have, *Call Waiting*. In fact, don't bother switching to catch a call when you're talking to him! Because he will just flat out hang up on you. He thinks it's rude and the truth is...*It is rude!* Do you think he'd believe me if I told him when I go home for Christmas, I tried to call him? *And couldn't get through for four months*? ...I don't think so!

I Fell In Love In Africa

I fell in love in Africa. His name is Moses and he is ten years old. His skin is as dark as the African night and his smile as captivating as the first star at twilight.

Moses lost his parents to AIDS. He lives in the Daughters of Charity orphanage with 150 other children. A place that I have visited only in motion pictures, where life is hard and comfort impossible to find. Kiwanga is a home run by Sister Rose. A woman who has devoted every waking moment of her adult life to being these children's only hope, their only champion against incredible odds.

On the first day there, I could only stay one hour. So afraid to touch anything, afraid of what disease I might catch, perhaps fearing their poverty was somehow contagious also. There I sat, petrified to embrace these children who needed a hand to hold as much as they needed clean clothes and nourishing food. Seeing the need in their eyes and unable to dig deep enough inside of myself to simply reach out my hand to them.

I left on that first day angry and disappointed in myself. I was hiding behind the meetings which needed to be held, the sites that needed to be seen and the shopping which needed to be done.

We went back the second day. I saw a young boy with a gaping wound on his leg and knew that I had at least the strength to clean and bandage his leg. Somewhere between the alcohol swab and the band-aid, this child smiled at me and I had to turn my head so he wouldn't see my tears…such a small thing to do for a child and such a gift of thanks.

On the third day we were asked to take a young woman to the hospital who was in the final stages of this disease which has taken so many lives. We lifted her out of the van to be admitted to the hospital where she died the next morning.

On the fourth day the children sang for us. And their voices were so pure, and the music so joyful that their poverty and their struggle was lost in its beauty. Perhaps when faith is all you have, the truth of it is somehow easier to find.

On the eighth day we bathed the younger children and cleaned all the cuts and sores of all the children. I realized that their unclean faces and wounds were not half as threatening to my life as the fear that I live with daily…the fear of risking my heart, of facing the part of life that my picket fence will not protect me from.

Uganda is a magical place. When I woke up in the mornings, it was to a sunrise of purple and gold spreading over the hills on the outskirts of Kampala. It is a place where the sky is so blue and the air so clear that you can smell the Sycamore tree several houses away.

Moses, thank you. I wish that I could tuck you in at night. I wish that I could make a plate of food so big that you would be full for days. I wish that I could tell you that you have awoken a place in my soul that has been asleep. I wish that I was there to make sure your wound is still clean.

Epilogue: I was asked to bless the food of a meal we provided for the children. Lord, please watch over these children and help them to grow old. Amen.

Watch Your Step!

Close your eyes. Pretend you are in your hometown for your twentieth high school reunion. You are trying to present an image of confidence, worldliness and sophistication. *The facade is going nicely until -- wham -- you are shanghaied by your own Mother!* Monty Hall (remember him? - - Let's Make a Deal) doesn't have a thing on my Mom. When you visit, you never know what lurks behind door number three. Example---Mom had been telling me about a play in Houston for no less than two months. "Can you go with me when you're here, what night can we go, I'll invite your sister?", etc. What the heck? I love the theater; I was going to be there anyway, so we made a date.

Silly me, thinking it would be just your average girls-night-out on the town when there is nothing even remotely average about my mother. At about noon, I asked her where our seats were for the play. "Seats? Well, we don't exactly have seats. Did I not mention to you that we were volunteers for the play"? "Excuse me?!", I ask dumbfounded. "Oh, I thought I had mentioned this to you," she says in her most innocent voice. "Mary (a long-time and very beloved family friend)? well, she needed volunteers, so I told her that you and I would help her out."

At this point I am still smiling but trying to keep my blood pressure in check. " I'm braced, Mom, tell me exactly what we do to "earn" these tickets?" "Well", she says sheepishly, "there are four jobs". "There are two ushers who show people to their seats and give out programs, one ticket taker and one 'Watch Your Step' person. The volunteers who get there first, get to choose their job". At this point I am grabbing my purse, running to the door while screaming, "Oh my gosh, just how soon do we have to get there to not be 'Watch Your Step'?"

We arrived at the theater well before the other volunteers. The stage manager began handing out assignments. I found myself waving my hand in the air, saying, "I want to be the ticket taker!" Here I am thinking I have the plum assignment. When the stage manager informs me I am to say, "Enjoy the Show" each time I tear the ticket in half. Hmm, door number one is "Enjoy the Show". Door number two is

"Watch Your Step". You choose. As you might imagine, the whole sophisticated image I had conjured up was in the toilet at this point. It was a religious play, so I felt it was perfectly appropriate to pray silently to myself, "Dear God, don't let anyone from my high school class be here!"

Of course I saw people I knew - - fate would not have it any other way. Even my own sister and niece giggled when they saw me (they had real seats in the front row). I would have been upset with them, but I figured they would get theirs on another day. There are many plays to come!

Epilogue: One week later, with a little perspective, I feel like a real heel for having pitched such a fit. Truth is, it wasn't so bad. What little embarrassment it did cause me has been justified by the subsequent gales of laughter I have enjoyed over this. And just think, my precious Mother has to live with the fact that these stories are now published.

I love you, Mom - Watch your step!

Sharp Shooter

My Mom is the best sport I know. She flew in yesterday at 2:00 PM and then volunteered to help me, feed and bid farewell to the eighteen children from Uganda I work with. I won't try to explain what it is like to corral and then order fast food for this many children. Suffice to say, it wasn't fast.

So, we're sitting around drinking coffee. Mom starts giving me, what I will call, her "backyard update." She launches into a tale of her wisteria. I am listening to her, dutifully wondering to myself just how long this report could take. I tuned in however, when I heard the words "sharp shooter", not knowing what a gunman had to do with wisteria. Come to find out, a sharp shooter is a slender, somewhat pointed shovel, used in gardening.

You see, Mom's wisteria was not blooming; it apparently had never bloomed. According to her gardening experts, the plant was just too darn content to create flowers. She was told she had to "upset the root system", which is where the sharp shooter came into play. Mom took the advice to heart. She went out into her yard, and began jamming the sharp shooter down into the ground about two feet from the actual plant. By gosh, this plant was going to produce flowers, if she had to uproot the whole thing to get them.

That's not the best part. Someone else told her, you could upset the plant by knocking it around a little. Please picture my very spry, but definitely Sr., Mom knocking her wisteria around with a stick. Mom and Jay live on a golf course, right on the fifth hole. In an effort to not be labeled completely nuts, she snuck out to her own backyard before the first tee time to shake up this plant. By this point in her tale, I have a full-blown visual picture of this covert wisteria operation.

An overwhelming sense of relief that I no longer lived at home was still washing over me, when she began the squirrel update. For a month now, she has had me convinced she is the first human being to have successfully outsmarted a squirrel. During our long distance conversations, she has detailed for me her homegrown squirrel deterrent. It was fairly simple, really. She painstakingly cut out the bottom of a two liter plastic cola bottle, put it upside down on her bird feeder pole and then greased the thing with cow udder balm. I have been thinking if this idea were to fly, she could become a millionaire soon. Well, the idea did not fly, because her squirrel did. Forget the squirrel having to shimmy past the greased-up bottle -- he just leapt from the ground right up to the bird feeder. Like millions of Americans who have gone down this anti-squirrel path, Mom now drinks her morning coffee and watches Mr. Squirrel performs his thieving acrobatics. The good news is her hands are nice and smooth from the cow udder balm.

Epilogue: Mom's own husband was skeptical about the Operation Wisteria. Imagine her righteousness when she actually found an article in the horticulture column of the newspaper about deadbeat wisteria. The article, of course, endorsed all the aforementioned methods of root abuse to make the thing bloom. *I am certain that when she reads this column, I will be receiving a copy of my own!*

On Venus We Have A Plan

Because men are from another planet…Pluto, Mars, whatever; they are on a completely different calendar and time schedule. It has to be their planet and ours are not rotating around the same sun. How else can one explain why they don't do anything on "female time?"

Although I don't have one of my own right now, I do dabble in relationships and observe dozens of others. Example: My friend, Alison, was having a dinner party on a Friday night for eight couples. That's a lot of work! They just moved into their new home six months ago, so there were many unfinished projects on the list. Alison is like many of us. Rather than span these projects over time, they were all scheduled for the week of the party. Her husband was going to be out of town for the week. This was a good thing. *I doubt he would have signed off on her faux painting four rooms and moving all the area rugs!*

You can only imagine the list waiting for Rob the morning he came home from his trip, the morning of the party. Moving furniture off the deck, some touch-up painting, hanging a few pictures… you get the idea. Rob, who is truly one of the greatest guys I know, did not say a word. But when I showed up mid-morning to help her get ready, where was Rob? He was out in the garage, underneath his car, changing the oil. *This was NOT on HER list!*

I had dinner with my friends, who just moved into their new home one week ago. The place looked incredible, as though they had lived there twenty years. Someone in that household was organizing this effort. My suspicion is it was not the gentleman with the USA Today in his hands when I walked in the door…it's just a guess.

Me? I left a voice mail for a man a yesterday, inviting him over for dinner with another couple for next weekend. My message told him to "pick a night" that worked for him and to let me know whenever. Oh my gosh! I didn't really mean "whenever"! I meant for him to look at his schedule and call me back last night! When waiting for a return call such as this, days become like dog years, one day might as well be seven, because that's what it feels like to us. He is probably just taking his sweet time, because he sees no reason not to. I, on the other hand, am becoming bitter.

I/we respect the differences between men and women, the different gifts and talents each bring to the table in a family or relationship. I have even noted men get in a much different 'gear' when in the work place. They prioritize, they get to meetings on time, and they "make things happen". This begs the question: just exactly who are these people sitting around in their boxers on the weekend?

Epilogue: Men, here's the deal! On Venus we have a plan, an agenda, a very delicate timetable. We, the women, have somehow been charged with moving things forward on a personal level. We have schedules fixated in our brains that AMTRAK could not rival. As an outside observer...*My advice would be "All aboard"!!*

The Answer Is: Size Matters

This morning, I weighed-in at my doctor's office! If I could have stripped down naked I would have, because in my world, one ounce matters. I begin removing articles...my shoes (16 oz.)...my sweatshirt (10 oz.)...even my watch (3 oz.). The medical profession, well, they are completely over the whole weigh-in trauma. E.g., phrases such as, "Hop on the scale". I have never hopped onto a scale in my life...because hopping is worth at least two extra pounds! Everyone knows you have to glide onto a scale, ideally holding onto some railing until your weight is completely balanced!

Another demonstration of their complete lack of sensitivity on this issue is when they yell your weight across the office, for some other nurse to put it on your chart. They are the same nurses that weighed us in grammar school I am sure. "Excuse me... could you please write that down on a piece of paper using disappearing ink and walk that over to them?"

Anyway, this newfound devotion to my diet started in a most unusual place -- a trip to Office Depot. I had dressed rather hurriedly for a meeting with a colleague of mine. Unbeknownst to me, the pair of black tights I grabbed were from a different "era", shall we say. They seemed to fit fine when I yanked them on and flew out the door. OK, so when I sat down in my car, I could tell something was not quite right. "Control top" doesn't normally mean cutting off your circulation!

Things that are too small just have a way of reacting to gravity. Can you imagine my sheer panic? I am standing in the checkout line. My tights started slipping down toward my knees? Fortunately I had on my long winter coat so I was covered and able to shuffle out of the store before the tights hit the floor.

Sizes and their impact on our psyche is a funny thing. I can recall with complete clarity the precise moment I decided to never again cram my foot in a shoe that was too small for the sake of my ego. I was standing at a photo-opportunity line in Washington, D.C. waiting to have my picture taken with President Reagan. I was sporting a pair of black, strappy high heels that matched my dress perfectly. The shoes looked fabulous; I was miserable. There are entire political careers built on making certain that someone such as the President of the United States never misses a beat. In these 'photo-op' lines, the President is equipped with an earpiece and as each person goes to shake his hand, he greets you by name. Even knowing that someone had literally just 'whispered my name in his ear' I was flattered and stunned all the same. Thank goodness these events are all about herding you through the line quickly! I am grateful there was no time for even a perfunctory, "how are you?" Although I can't be one hundred percent certain, I am pretty sure that the only words I would have had for the President of the Free World would have been, "my feet are killing me". I made a pact with my feet that night and I have never traded comfort for style since then.

Most would say only women demonstrate this type of vanity. Yet I have seen men display the same aversion to admitting what size they wear. "Honey, I like this shirt, but I don't wear an Extra Large... it's supposed to fit tight!" Wives and girlfriends all over America are replying with, "OK, I'll take it back and exchange it for a smaller size", as they cut the tags off and place it in the aforementioned gentleman's closet.

Epilogue: Let's open a clothing store. Let's call it "Fantasy". Nothing in the store will have a tag on it. You just run around holding the clothes up to you and decide whether or not it looks like the right size. You try it on and if it works, you take it home, a happy person. I'll take truisms for $500 Alex...and the question is: "Does size really matter?"

In the Beginning

In the beginning, there was the rotary phone. From that phone, man created touch-tone phones with long cords. And the long cord phone begat the cordless phone…which begat the cell phone. "What are you doing?", asked the man, after I picked up the phone last night. I should have never grabbed the thing, but I thought I knew who it was. In 1970, I would have had no problem answering his question. I would have been sitting in the only chair in my kitchen the phone cord reached.

As it happens, I was taking a bubble bath. While I would have shared this with my Mother (I thought it was her calling me back), I was not willing to admit this to a man I believed was going to ask me out on a date. I froze in place and answered the question, "Not much".

That's the problem with lying in general. You start spinning a web you can't exit from later with any grace at all. He begins chatting about his week, how busy he's been, how sorry he is that he hasn't called. Normally I would have been delighted to hear about the minutia of his life…but the water is turning cold around me…and the bubbles are disappearing. There is a very slight drip from the faucet, which in the quiet sounds like a gushing stream. I am trying to plug the drip with my big toe, so he can't hear the water…while simultaneously trying to keep the phone dry, to avoid electrocution.

"I was actually calling …." "Good, he's going to ask me out now, so I can say yes, hang up, and get out of this now frigid water. " ….to see if you had Marianne's address". Great, that's just marvelous. Not only am I being "dissed", I have now "pruned" myself in vain. I was trying to calculate how I get out of the bathtub without making any noise, to get him his lousy address. Don't worry; it did finally occur to me that, because there was no invitation forthcoming, I could call the man back, which I did.

Thanks to cell phones, call forwarding, call waiting, and cordless phones, we can be virtually anywhere, doing anything, when someone calls us. In circa 1970, the question should have been, "What were you doing before you abandoned whatever it was to go to the kitchen or your bedroom to answer the phone?" Phones used to be an anchor of sorts. My poor Mother never had a private conversation because anytime she got on the phone; I would become "needy" and stand right next to her until she hung up. No wonder she doesn't gossip!

When I was growing up, a family with more than two phone jacks was considered very well-to-do. Having a "children's line" was considered manna from heaven. A busy signal simply meant you would try them back later...it was not cause for alarm or frustration. The phone company knows their public. Now, for only seventy-five cents they will re-dial a number for you if it's busy. Gosh, I'm probably among the top ten percent of users/abusers of phone technology and even I'm not buying into that feature. They got me once out of sheer confusion, but I get it now.

Epilogue: Makes me wonder. Did phones become more important because our worlds expanded off the block we live on? Or did the block we live on become less important, because of far reaching phones?

Stereo Parents

It was 10:00 AM on a Saturday. My Mom and stepfather, Jay, had just picked me up from the airport in Wheeling, West Virginia. We were there to celebrate my Uncle Al's and Aunt Janet's fiftieth wedding anniversary, which, given today's marital statistics, should be applauded! At this point I had already been up five hours, as I had to drop, Champ, my dog, off at a friend's before leaving. My mood was, how shall I say, "pleasant challenged." So I ask you, when was the last time you rode in the back seat of a small car with your parental units for an extended period of time? All I know is, for 90 minutes there was not a break in the chatter from up front... *"You missed the turn. No, I didn't. Where are the windshield wipers in this car? You're not watching for the exit. Yes, I am. There it was,"* and so on. I would say that they were dialoguing, but that would imply one of them stopped talking to allow the other one to speak. It was more like 'stereo parents.'

What seemed like four lifetimes later, we arrive at the hotel. I go to get out of the car...I can't open the door...It won't open...it's childproof...how disgustingly ironic. I am thirty-eight years old, out of town with the folks and basically trapped in a sky blue Mercury, having a panic attack. The 'parental stereo' starts up again, this time with instructions on how to open a car door. "Oh, my gosh, Mom, it won't open, just please let me out of here!"

We check in, with full intent of sharing a room for one night. It took all of about five minutes to evaluate the situation and ask for my own room. Twenty minutes later, we left for the first of three scheduled feedings. Not that it doesn't suit me just fine, but have you ever noticed families cannot manage a get together without food being present? It must help to numb the senses somehow!

We arrive at the first reunion. Cousins who I haven't seen in years -- no more braces, no more long braids. We hug and kiss. My Mother takes the first of five rolls of film. We chat, we leave.

We hop in the childproof auto to go back to the hotel to shower and change for the actual celebration. The dinner begins at 6:00 PM, but we have to be there at 4:30 PM for pictures. I remember a time when our family dinners began at 8:00 PM. This was during the brief period when no one, young or old, went to bed before 9:00 in the evening.

Anyway, the photographer miraculously memorizes everyone's name and, more amazing still, their family affiliation. We are being grouped and regrouped, standing on blocks, sitting on armchairs and smiling. My cousin, Cathy, puts on her best camera smile and says to me under her breath, "We have to smile and pretend we know each other".

Epilogue: I confess - - the whole weekend was quite fun. All those childhood memories flooding back, seeing glimpses of people we love and people we miss in their eyes and in their smiles. I find myself loving these relatives of mine, without ever having spent longer than a week at a time with them. *No matter how many years go by, we are irrevocably connected by the tie that binds -- we are family!*

Who Wants to Be a Millionaire?

So, who wants to be a millionaire? Now that's a pretty silly question! Or at least I thought so, until I met with my bookkeeper last Saturday. Odd as this may seem I purchase lottery tickets when the pot gets big, but never look to see if I have won. Some people argue the lottery is a complete waste of hard earned money. Certainly this is true in my case. I stuff them in my receipt drawer, where they remain until the expiration date has long since passed. Maybe it is because intellectually I know what the odds really are. Maybe it's because I don't want to be a millionaire. That's a scary thought. My bookkeeper reprimanded me for this ridiculous habit and then suggested we look at the old tickets, to see if any of them were winners. "You know, just to see." I quickly likened this to some modern equivalent of a torture chamber and proceeded to feed the tickets into my new shredder.

My dear friend, Ruth, lives in a state where no lottery exists. Therefore, when the pot gets truly worth winning, she will call and ask me to buy a couple of quick picks for her. Unlike when I buy them for myself, I then tape the tickets to my fridge and am very diligent about checking the winning numbers. One morning when I was checking the results, I had a revelation I had to share with Ruth immediately. I call it a revelation; it was truly a confession. I began thinking about how I would feel if she actually won the thing? Am I a nice enough person to feel good about handing over a winning ticket? No, I am not. Ruth and I discussed this for about two seconds and employed the fifty-fifty rule for this little game. This sounded like a lot more fun to both of us. Who wants to shop for a living alone anyway?

Really, I have a lot more fun watching other folks trying to win a million dollars than I've ever had buying a lotto ticket. I admit it; I have actually been sucked into this new American craze. It is a very cunning game. They throw in questions my nieces Julia, Alicia and Kristen (none of who are old enough to drive) could answer, laced with trivia that no one has ever delved into. My personal favorite, "What is the name of the dog on the Cracker Jack box?"

I don't know about you, but the only time Cracker Jacks even cross my mind is when I'm at a ballgame. But even the beloved song 'Take Me Out to the Ballgame' does not include the name of the dog for goodness sake! So there Hugh and I sit, listening to the seconds tick by, while this guy, like us, is totally stumped by the question worth $32,000. Can't you just imagine what it's like to think if you had only, just once, glanced at the box, instead of worrying about the prize, you might be a millionaire? This nice gentleman then calls his Father for a "life line". He, too, is stumped. I'm sure this did a lot for their relationship! As it turns out, the dog's name is BINGO. No---it can't be---that's the farmer's dog!

Epilogue: Since I have admitted to tuning into this show occasionally, I want to say in self-defense I did not watch one day of the O.J. Simpson trial. I watched the chase, but... **everybody watched the chase, didn't they?**

All Over Shapers

When I am "steppin' out" in my finest, I do not want to feel like I am held together by spit and luck, as was the case yesterday. It was near midnight Saturday when I realized I was missing a vital piece of my Sunday ensemble. While laying out Hugh's and my respective suits and accessories for the big event, it dawned on me I had no pantyhose "in stock". We had to be at the church by noon the next day, so stopping by a department store on the way was not an option. You need only think twenty-four-hour-superstore to figure out where I went to resolve my dilemma. *By the by, pollsters looking for a perfect cross-section of the American public need only stand at the exit door of a superstore at midnight to get their random sample.*

When searching for pantyhose in an up-scale department store, I am always overwhelmed by the choices available. You've got your daytime sheer, your nighttime sheer, your reinforced toe and your sandal foot variety. Then, to make matters even more confusing, they take all these hose alternatives and add a different panty to create ten more options. This is the land where no man has gone before! Pantyhose *figure-busters!!*

Basically, the manufacturers have taken the much-dreaded girdle of the 20th century and disguised it as pantyhose. Those of us born prior to 1970 recognize a girdle when we see one. They are not fooling us with this "slims your tummy, hips and thighs with comfort and fit" rhetoric. We know that when you voluntarily displace ten percent of your body mass, it is not, in fact, going to be comfortable. This is beside the point really. When you're shopping for pantyhose in a place that also carries yard fertilizer, your choices are extremely limited! I purchased the one and only pair of black hose available in my size and went home, hoping they would work. I didn't have time to examine what type of pantyhose I had bought. Which is good, since I would have had nightmares if I'd known they were an *"all-over shaper!"*

The next morning, while getting dressed, Hugh complained his dress shirt collar is too tight. I wanted to toss him my "shapers", tell him to pour himself in and then talk to me. I finally coaxed the pantyhose on, put on my suit dress and stared in the mirror. About that time, Hugh flipped on the overhead light, which is when I realized this suit needed a slip as well. There was no time to run back to the store, I had to improvise. I came up with a black half-slip I wear with longer winter skirts and pulled it on. The slip worked perfectly, except for the four inches of lace hanging below the hem. There was no time to slipstitch the slip and I didn't want to actually cut the length off. So I simply took the elastic waistband and tugged it under and through my bra. In short, I was experiencing a *lingerie meltdown!*

Epilogue: We had been anticipating this event with some nervousness, as Hugh and I were standing up for his Father's wedding. I don't know what Hugh was thinking during the ceremony, but as the preacher was saying a blessing on their marriage, I was praying that my slip and my pantyhose wouldn't fall to my ankles before we got back down the aisle. Yet another example of an answered prayer.

Cooking for Dummies

It is hard to form the perfect biscuit when most of the dough is stuck to your hands. "Cover your surface and knead gently", the recipe states. This is one of several examples where there is a widespread gap between what you read and what you get. I knew I had missed some vital, yet unwritten, code of cooking. So I did what I always do in a sticky situation --- I tried to call my Mother.

I reached for the cordless phone and as I punched in the numbers I was inadvertently clogging up the keypad with the dough from my hands. *Of course*, I should have washed my hands first but the whole bowl of dough was stuck to them, which would have meant sacrificing the entire batch of biscuits to my cooking naiveté. I then got out a paper towel to clean the dough out of the keypad. I only managed to spread the gooey substance to the rest of the phone. At this point, I abandoned the concept of saving the batter and scrubbed my hands, but not without first covering the sink faucets with my "easy to make" raw biscuit dough!

Feeling confident I had the dough under control, I went for the phone a second time. I was dialing just fine, but there was something sticky on my earlobe. The dough was now covering one of my fake diamond earrings! I then had to immerse the earring in jewelry cleaner made only for real jewelry. My once-silver earrings are now a grayish color. The cost of these biscuits just rose by fifteen bucks!

This was now my third attempt to reach my long distance cooking advisor. "Did you cover your hands in flour *before* you started kneading the dough?" Mom queries. *"No, I did not!" "Why didn't I do this?" "Because the directions skipped that part, that's why."* Although the overused adage "Never assume anything..." bores me to tears, it does make a good point. The writers of recipes are so skilled at their craft that they tend to omit vital information such as: do I cover this casserole or not? Do I cook the noodles before or do they cook while in the oven? What, what, what do you do with *"those parts"* inside the turkey? And the most popular omission of all: "Bake for 45 minutes." Bake at what temperature? My oven has a temperature range of 500 degrees. So trust me, I need more detail!

57

It all looks so easy when someone else cooks. I have watched numerous chefs on television. Dozens of real-life men and women chop, simmer and boil with no mishaps. I am fascinated by their ability to slice, knead and dice. I am equally as amazed they are not wearing half of their raw materials. Why don't the recipe publishers take a page from the computer manuals and include a section on trouble shooting? I need a section on how you get eggshell out of cake mix. There should also be a section on source materials. I flat-out need someone to tell me olives can be purchased pre-sliced, before I cut off a finger. One more idea: instead of dividing recipes by appetizers, desserts and entrées, how about breaking them down into beginning, intermediate and advanced?

Epilogue: I finally abandoned the dough kneading fiasco and went for drop biscuits. It was several hours later that I returned to the kitchen for K.P.. Hardened dough, like any mistake left unattended, is a not an easy chore to face. *Can someone please publish "Cooking for Dummies", complete with chapters on stain removal and first aid?!*

Double Exposure

Cathy, my first cousin, my stepbrother, Lance, and I all got married for the first time in the same year. All three of us are over forty years old, which makes it even more bizarre. My Mom and my stepfather, Jay, attended all three weddings. They helped out with all the things that really no one else is willing to do for you. They also helped out in a way that for years our families wished they wouldn't...*They took pictures!*

Mom likes to capture special events on film. She is an enthusiastic and determined taskmaster when it comes to getting group shots. Only the matriarch of a family can make you put down your food or leave a conversation to snap a group she hasn't yet organized. She is, in more ways than one, the family historian. All of us who are related to her have learned that, out of the dozens of pictures taken, there will be only one or two that are "frame-able". The rest are just a very thorough documentation of who was present at any event we have. These pictures will have their proper place in history I'm sure.

My Mother is a very organized woman in all things. Especially when it comes to the distribution of these historical shots. Duplicates are always made. The originals are kept in a place I never want to see. Copies are then sent to the appropriate person or persons. If you're lucky, you will receive a picture-by-picture description over the phone before you ever receive the package.

I had already received the package of candid and posed shots from our wedding. As always, they made me smile, realizing the love and effort that goes into this many bad shots. I could smile...I knew the professional pictures were on the way.

Imagine my panic when Mom called from Texas the weekend of Lance and Xiaohong's wedding and let slip that she and Jay were the photographers for their special day. I inquired as diplomatically as I could, "Is anyone else taking pictures?"

Flash forward two weeks. Mom and Jay are at the store picking up the prints from Lance's wedding. They are looking through the rolls of film when they realized they had entered a whole new realm of picture-taking snafus. Some how, some way, a roll had been double exposed. An entire role of film from our wedding had been used to take pictures at Lance and Xiaohong's ceremony as well!

There we all were; the two happy couples. Though the events were six weeks and eight hundred miles apart, we had been captured in the same frames! Pictures of all of our friends laughing together, poignant shots of me alone...with Lance's image faded into the background. You get the 'picture'.

We still don't know how this double loop happened, though Mom and Jay have devoted hours of discussion trying to retrace their steps. I honestly don't know how you can mistake a finished roll of film for a new one when the tail is embedded inside. Did they happen to have a pair of tweezers handy when loading the film for the second time? What we do know is that the initial frustration has faded into weeks of laughter for all of us.

Epilogue: I wouldn't trade these tales for any amount of money. My perfectly imperfect family is what makes this world make sense to me. I feel as though we have finally caught the essence of our family on film.

Thank God For You

My Mother laughs at herself while she's telling a funny story! So do I! We amuse ourselves in a way that must strike many as a private joke with no real punch line and 'm quite certain some must think us very odd indeed. It is my mom who taught me how to find humor in my own eccentricities and shortcomings: a tool that has given me great strength. Since she allows me such license with her sometimes-embarrassing stories, I wanted to share with you some of my Mother's other attributes.

I have a quilt on my bed my Mom made from the fabric of my dresses I wore growing up. Each square, meticulously sewn together, reminds me of a now-distant memory of my childhood. They represent the hours she spent sewing for my sisters and me. I didn't know then what a labor of love this was until now. Every day if I look at the quilt, I understand more and more about a Mother's love.

Our childhood was complete with the chaos and the challenges all families face. Through it all, we learned the importance of "family". While we each have different styles and different attitudes we are bound by a history; a curiosity about things beyond our reach; and a belief that life is very much worth living.

When I was a teenager, I tested my Mother's patience and understanding. There were several years of reckless behavior, during a time when she was fighting her own battles. She persevered. I grew up. That time in our lives binds us together, as closely as allies on a battlefield. As a young woman, I came to her with the wreckage of my personal life. She held me in her arms and cried with me. She taught me about compassion and about unconditional love.

When I moved to Atlanta, years ago, she was determined to help me make my apartment a home. She came for a long weekend not to be entertained, but to sew curtains for me. She can work steadily on one project until it is complete which is regrettably not one of my strong suits!

When I was married, she helped me celebrate my happiness with every detail and every major decision in a way that only a Mother is able to. She was the person who had to tell me how many inches my wedding dress needed to actually zip. She delivered this news as she has so many facts of life over the years…without judgment.

I have watched my mom over the years, coming to know and respect her as a woman of great substance. She has given her grandchildren, her children, her husband, her friends her energy and, the most precious gift of all, her time. She has created memories we all treasure. She has launched traditions to help to define who we are in this world. She is about kindness and finding joy in the simplest of acts---the smallest of treasures.

I never knew my Mom's Mother, but she lives inside of me. I feel closer to her than some people I have walked on this earth with. Because I know the gifts that give me the greatest joy are the very gifts my Grandmother passed down to my mom. I sometimes stare at Grandmother's picture and know I will meet her one-day, hear her laughter and know that I am home!

Epilogue: *Happy Mother's Day, Mom –thank God for you!!* Written in honor of Betty Brouthers and in loving memory of Mildred Stender.

Salt in the Wound

You've heard the old adage, "rubbing salt into a wound?" Like me, you probably never intended to find out what this felt like, when applied literally. Exfoliate: The new millennium's definition of the fountain of youth. When your old skin becomes tired and haggard...simply remove it. *You can get to this new layer of skin chemically, surgically or through the most popular method, over-the-counter miracle crèmes!*

When confronted with these creams, I have the sales resistance of a five-year-old at a gumball machine. I go to get a pedicure leave with whatever new product they have acquired since my last visit. This week's product was guaranteed to exfoliate your skin to baby-like softness. The women in the salon regaled me with stories of how smooth their skin felt. So I bought their stories and the product. Like all exfoliates, this product was to be used while bathing. I set the stage perfectly in my luxurious garden tub. I had bubbles, candles, big fluffy towels and an air pillow. Hugh was downstairs engrossed in a computer project. I put on some soft music and was thoroughly enjoying my escape.

I luxuriated about five minutes before I became anxious to try my new product that would give me back my youthful skin. I should have known something would go awry when I accidentally dropped the miracle crème into my warm bath water and the instructions washed off. Because I do not generally read and follow instructions, I felt safe in proceeding on gut instinct. I opened the package with my teeth and began rubbing this miracle lotion all over my body. I'm not sure what I was expecting, but this potion was coarse and oily. In fact, it felt very much like a combination of rock salt and suntan oil!

Quite suddenly, the soothing miracle lotion turned into a sheath of pain. I had, without thinking, applied my miracle oil to a still open wound on my elbow. It took all of one second for me to determine the source of my agony. I tried to rinse the salt out of my wound, but, by this time, the entire bath was filled with the stuff. I made matters worse when I went to brush the hair out of my eyes...and got the salt in them. *I had to get out of this tub of pain!* Note at this point my body was "moisturized" from head to toe so trying to get enough traction to get out of the tub was a challenge. I did finally manage to slither out onto the bath mat, whereby I wrapped myself in towels and allowed my childlike tears to flow. It was at this point that I noticed my upper torso was covered in hives. I am allergic to suntan oil. Surely, surely, I had not just applied suntan oil to my entire body?

Epilogue: I admit it. I was preparing for a romantic evening with Hugh, inspired by my baby soft skin. Instead, we spent the evening applying cortisone and first aid cream to my body, while I winced in pain. *The moral of the story is -- if your skin fits, wear it!*

Welcome to the Net, Mom!

My Mother has now gone "on-line". I never really felt like Mom and I suffered from a "digital divide" since Ma Bell has kept she and I quite well connected for years now. As her E-mails flood my in-box, I am incredulous at just how much news I have been missing out on!

I have been encouraging Mom for months to get E-mail but honestly never dreamt it would actually happen. There is absolutely nothing intuitive about setting up E-mail, especially when someone is jumping into this technology midstream. I've been on the Internet four years and I still struggle with how to attach a document.

What I'm trying to say is, Mom did not simply buy or download a software program, install the program, plug in her phone and begin sending mail. *She is a smart woman! She knows when to ask for help!* My sister, Diane, and her entire family are extremely computer literate and as luck would have it (didn't say which kind of luck) they live only twenty miles from Mom and Jay. Suffice to say that Diane and her gang have spent quite a bit of "quality time" with mom over the several weeks!

While they are worlds apart in terms of speed of delivery, the United States Post Office and the Internet do have a couple of common features. Technology aside, if you've got the wrong E-mail address, your correspondence is not going to arrive safely. And because on the Internet you don't have friendly neighbors who know who you are and where you live, your mail can occasionally get lost in the great on-line abyss.

For instance: mom has been writing to some random woman who happens to have an E-mail address one number "off" from mine. For at least a week she has regaled this perfect stranger with tales of running into my best friend, an update on the nieces and nephews as well as her general health. The random woman, confused by my mother's E-mails finally replied to her in the curt manner that only Internet users can employ -- "don't know you!"

Mom and I were on the phone trying to unravel the mystery of the lost letters when she received this E-mail from "Sharon with no zero". After we stopped laughing hysterically at this woman's economy of words, I attempted to teach her how to "forward" Internet mail.

Here's a tip: **DO NOT** tutor your parents on how to use E-mail via the phone long distance. I have absolutely no idea who received those forwarded letters ... but again, it was not me! **Perhaps Mom will be hearing back from whoever it was soon.**

For years, my siblings and I have received in the mail clipped newspaper or magazine articles our Mother believes we will find of interest. I fear with all my heart the day she learns how to browse the obituaries on-line! That day is coming...soon...I can feel it! I haven't even told her about on-line greeting cards as I know this particular site will be met with great enthusiasm!

Epilogue: Truth is, I'm proud of my Mom for embracing this new technology. It would have been so easy for her to let this particular mode of communication pass her by. But then again, not much has ever gotten past my Mom. **I only *thought* that it did!**

Home Olympics

Hugh and I are riveted by the Olympic competition. We sit on our respective couches, cheering on these icons of Americana athletics…marveling at their skill…their tenacity…their physiques. We are proud…we are enthusiastic…we are officially depressed. The gulf between the athlete and the spectator is almost too much to bear. I am sporting a too big sweatshirt and pajama bottoms…Husband Hugh is wearing the shirt he wore to dinner and some stretchy pants…we are eating ice cream. *It isn't pretty!*

As with any other sport shown on television, the Olympic competition requires you take care of any and all personal business during commercial breaks. The television coverage moves around so quickly from sport to sport, you could miss the pinnacle moment if you leave your couch too soon. In an effort to combat our depression, we have come up with our own Home Olympics.

1st Event…The dirty-dish-and-water-refill race. This takes place in the kitchen venue; the concentration required is mind-boggling. Hugh must take his plate to the sink, rinse it, get a clean glass, fill it with ice, locate and pick up the inevitably dropped ice cubes, fill the glass with water and return to the couch within three minutes. I am proud to report that Hugh has achieved his personal best in this sport, winning a Gold!

2nd Event… The dog-walking challenge. Can I rally our dog, Champ, get his leash on, take him to his street corner and get him to come back in all within five minutes? If you don't complete your mission and the dog barks to go out within two hours, you are eliminated.

3rd Event…One of our more intricate games is the laundry race. This includes running upstairs (bonus points received if you actually run), dumping the dirty clothes into the transport hamper, running back downstairs, sorting the clothes and starting the first load of darks on the correct temperature.

4th Event…During the more extended sports such as the triathlon, our competitions become more complex. There is a dishwasher contest that includes unloading the dishes sitting in there for two days, plus rinsing and loading the pile that has been left in the sink. Unanticipated challenges include dishes not fully dried and/or hard to remove food particles!

5th Event...Hugh is competing today in the checkbook reconciliation category. He must enter and balance all of our personal expenditures within three commercial breaks. He is a contender for at least a Silver medal in this heady competition.

6th & Final Event...Last, but not least, the phone relay. In this event you must return a call, get the required information from caller A and get off the phone with them, make a second call(s) to caller B, C, D or whomever, then pass that information on to the necessary person(s), all in six minutes. This is my event...I own this sport. *I am going for the Gold!*

Epilogue: We can't all be athletes, but I am going to see if I can find a bathing suit like the ones worn by the USA women's swim team. *It will be the first competition suit I've seen that covers your thighs!*

Life Compass

Yesterday was a gorgeous, clear winter day and my friend, Jim, stopped by to see me at the business we own. Hugh was there too so I asked Jim if he could run me home to pick up some things I'd forgotten. "Plus...you could see our new house!," I added as though this held any interest for Jim whatsoever. It was a great day for driving and Jim is a good guy so he agreed to take me home.

I realized about five minutes into the drive to my house that perhaps I had issued the invite to quickly. I began issuing disclaimers as soon as I recalled the messy kitchen and general disarray of the house when we left that morning. "We haven't had much time for housekeeping. The Christmas wreath is off the mantle, but it's lying against the couch. I don't think I loaded the dishwasher this morning before we left. The icicle lights are still on the back porch. My office looks like a paper recycling plant. Other than that, the house looks great."

Jim is a diplomat at heart so he politely rebuffed my comments with "I don't care Sharon, I just want to see your new house." I tried to take him at his word. But when we got to the house and showed him around, he asked what I know to be code for, "My gosh your house is messy." He stood in the middle of our den and asked, *"How long have you lived here again?"* The sub-text of this question is... *"No way can you get this much stuff crammed into one house in one year!"* **Well, yes you can...and we did!**

That is why I woke up this morning with a personal pledge to get organized for once and for all. I am starting with my office and I have enlisted a tool that I'm certain will set my life in order nicely. It's called "Your Weekly Compass", with a sub-title of "What Matters Most." It divides your world into "Roles and Goals", with four sub-categories: Physical, Social/Emotional, Mental, and Spiritual. The compass is to be filled out weekly or daily, as a reminder to take care of first things first. A concept that I struggle with daily!

The makers of this tool even give you examples under each category, to make it easier to begin. The first category is "Physical"...their example is "Nature Walk 3X." I suspect they don't consider running to the bathroom in-between phone calls qualifies as a nature walk. But that's as close as I've come lately. Under each category, they have the word "Role". They provide you with examples of important roles in our hectic lives, such as being a good spouse or friend. I agree that these roles should come first, so I move on to the next step. I am eager to find a system to help me to be a well-rounded person again.

Under each role, they have empty lines entitled "Q11 Goals." Although they provide you with an example of a Q11, I still don't get what it stands for. So here I sit in the midst of my insanity, ignoring what matters most and obsessing about what the heck Q11 means. I cannot believe this was the manufacturer's intent.

E**pilogue**: I ordered my Compass Cards in 1998. I just haven't gotten around to it until today, which could explain many things I don't care to think about. I've spent the last hour excavating old boxes, to see if this stupid Compass came with directions. *Losing the directions for a Life Compass, how very ironic!*

The Question With No Answer Question

If I could just stop our lawn and my husband Hugh's hair from growing we would have a conflict-free marriage. The length and grooming of these two living, flourishing, entities remains an ongoing debate in our home. It is the genesis for many of our more heated discussions.

These discussions always start off as fairly benign.

"Honey, the grass looks a little long from all that rain, are you planning on cutting it soon?", I inquire with a saccharine sweet smile on my face. "I've got to wait until the ground dries, or the mower will leave ruts. I'll handle it as soon as I can", Hugh responds with an equally forced smile.

Now, *IF* I could just stop right there and walk away! *IF* I could just not say…*"When do you think that will be?"*

That's it! I have just asked my husband's favorite type of question. Which is -- *The Question With No Answer Question*. I have trapped him into making a commitment, based on the unknown forces of nature. He knows from experience, there is no right answer to these seemingly harmless queries of mine. He could respond with "I don't know", an honest but unacceptable answer. Or he could give me a contrived time, which I would attempt to hold him to, even under a hurricane watch. Sometimes he chooses to remain silent, which Hugh mistakenly considers a safe bet.

Will men ever learn, silence is to women what fire is to gasoline? Silence is only a winner for rhetorical questions thrown out to unsuspecting males, such as, "I wonder if I'd look good as a brunette?"

When I know I am behaving in a neurotic fashion but can't seem to stop myself, I write things down, so that I can see how ridiculous I'm being. Toward that end, I have composed the lawn-mowing and hair-cutting creeds, based on my innermost feelings on these matters.

I believe the lawn should be cut weekly, whether it needs it or not. I believe the lawn can be cut whether the grass is wet or not. I believe newcomers to any neighborhood will be judged by the length of their grass. I believe if you want to bad enough, you can cut the lawn before it actually starts raining (although *never* during lightening, for safety reasons). And, here's the kicker…I believe lawn mowing can be fun, if one can find the right attitude.

I believe hair should be confined to the scalp area and promptly removed from all erroneous spots, such as the neck or ears. I believe hair should be cut when the first signs of a comb-over are noticed. I believe unruly hair reflects poorly on the spouse/girlfriend/mother. I believe haircuts are a great Saturday morning activity. I believe if you don't want to pay for a salon cut (i.e. appointment time), then you should bring the sports page …and enjoy waiting in line.

Epilogue: These over-the-top beliefs are unfortunately not limited to the lawn and Hugh's hair. I have several unspoken creeds relating to things that are either beyond anyone's control (least of all mine) or are none of my business. *I'd hate to think we could not find marital harmony before Hugh goes bald or the grass just dies!*

Never Let' em See You Sweat

Husband Hugh has a meeting tonight. It conflicts with the final three holes of the The Masters golf tournament. He has asked me, "Please tape the ending, if you would". However nonchalantly the request was made, I knew better than to take it lightly. I have the tournament recording in not one VCR, but two, as I write this column.

I love to watch golf tournaments too, but not for the game. As a card carrying Drama Queen, I am mesmerized by how these golfers keep a grip on their emotions, under that level of stress. These men and women can nail a put from thirty feet away and the most you're going to get out of them is an arm in the air. They can lose a tournament by one stroke and they just tuck their chin to their chest and walk off the green. Keep in mind this one stroke could have cost them tens of thousands of dollars.

If that happened to me, or any Drama Queen, we would drop to our knees and roll around in the grass sobbing. A chin tuck is for when you lose a game of ten-dollar BINGO. A chin tuck is appropriate when your child comes in second in the 100-yard dash. A chin tuck is when you miss the Lucky Lotto by only three out of five numbers. How do they keep it together like that? You get more of a reaction than this from me, when I run my hose before leaving the house.

Here's the other thing about golfers that fascinates me. They have taken the "never let 'em see them sweat" adage to a whole new level. These people literally do not sweat at all! They walk miles in the hot sun, sporting long pants and the occasional layered look. Still not one drop of perspiration streams down their face. They remain calm, cool, collected to the point of annoying. I can begin to perspire by just imagining I'm wearing that sweater vest in eighty degrees. This is just not natural. The only logical explanation is they all have some a type of hypoactive golf-gland.

There is no other sport on this earth where the rules of conduct are as important as the complex rules of the game. My brother, Jeff, is an avid golfer and officiates some tournaments as well. I am careful not to ask for too many details about these rules, for fear he might explain them to me. Keeping in step with his golf colleagues, Jeffrey is the epitome of self-restraint. Although we come from the same gene pool, you would swear we weren't related. My theory is all of those self-control, self-discipline, self- fill-in-the-blank genes were distributed equally amongst my three siblings, before I was ever even born. It is a theory that works for me, no matter how steeped in denial it might be.

Epilogue: Hugh came home a while ago and turned on the VCR. Of course the tape started skipping and dragging, as Murphy's Law would dictate. Can you imagine how impressed he was, when I pulled out the second tape? I garnered major brownie points in that moment which I will cash in later. Perhaps I have learned a thing or two about this highly mental game through pure osmosis. The great golfer, Bobby Jones, once said, "*Competitive golf is played mainly on a five-and-a-half-inch course, the space between your ears.*" **See, that's why you never see 'em sweat!**

Basement Blizzard

We've already had our first "snow" this year. It fell just last week. A soft layer of white, which would have looked absolutely magnificent if hadn't been inside our basement!

Home improvement, ain't it great? The "snow" powder is a byproduct of Tom's (my father-in-law) effort to undo something we had just paid someone last week to do. Tom disappeared into our basement with a facemask and an electric sander. He emerged two hours later looking like Father Christmas.

I was too afraid to go downstairs and look at the fall-out effect and for good reason. When I finally descended slowly into the basement with a single wet tile on Saturday, I almost fainted! Who knew that sanding sheetrock compound from Hardy Board could cause a blizzard?

This whole home improvement thing has been an amazing learning experience for me. As with any new frontier, there are hard lessons to be learned.

Lesson One: Don't think for one second just because you are writing the check that you have the power. As the American work force evolved from skilled laborers to white-collar workers, the supply and demand economics of home improvement is definitely skewed in favor of the folks actually doing the work. You can attempt to schedule them, but basically they show up whenever they want to. Our sheetrock man called Hugh at 10 PM one night to say he was coming by to start our job. Husband Hugh told him it was too late. Huge mistake. He voiced his displeasure in a very passive-aggressive manner by not calling or showing up for a solid week. I even left our tile-man syrupy sweet voicemails, saying he could show up in the middle of the night if he wanted to, but my efforts were in all in vain. He was punishing us for not working within his schedule.

Lesson Two: If you miss a deadline, by even a day, for Phase I, Phases II, III and IV fall disproportionately behind schedule. Construction time-lines can be likened to building a house of cards. The "house" plan is held together by such delicate balance that the slightest change in events can cause the whole structure to tumble.

Here's a word you don't want to hear when executing a home improvement plan -- "*Back-Order*"! The only people who are more evasive and less specific than the sub-contractors themselves are the vendors selling you supplies. We currently have a toilet, an order of bull-nose tile and several faucet heads floating around in "back-order land". There's no need to call and check on the arrival date of these critical pieces. I've been advised I will know they arrive when they show up and are delivered. OK, I'll just wait then!?

Lesson Three: Comparison-shopping is not part of the construction game. You must talk to neighbors and friends who have already "been there, done that" to figure out a ballpark price before you ever make a call. Both the sheetrock guy and the tile man came to our house to quote **AND to start the job right now!** They were visibly shocked when we told them we'd have to think about it. Hugh and I were amused and annoyed by their smugness. That was before we knew that we were hugely unimportant to them.

Epilogue: You might recall that the downstairs bathroom was on my project calendar to be finished mid-September. I have now adjusted my expectations and am hoping the toilet is installed by 2003. The whole fiasco is turning into a two-for-one nightmare; install a bathroom and get a divorce for fewer than two thousand dollars.

Greatest Gifts

There are days when I get so sad for those in my life, those whose pain I cannot fix or erase and for the inevitable journey towards goodbyes.

I took our beloved Champ to the doggie clinic last week, because he hasn't seemed himself in so long. The veterinarian gave me some medicine to put in his tired eyes. I think it was more for me than for Champ. The good doctor knew I needed to feel like I could help him in some small way. Champ's and my morning rituals are now slowed by his decaying eyesight, his hind legs that hurt when he runs, and the fact that he just doesn't really hear anymore.

Being with this dog for thirteen years has given me such comfort and such purpose. I can barely stand to watch, as he tries to find me with the one sense that has not failed him...his sense of smell. When he finally does sniff his way to me, I am overcome with the need to pick him up and hold him. I want desperately for him to know that I'm just not ready for him to go. And yet somehow I know that my sweet Champ is tired. So I pray that when his time does come, that I am able to say goodbye while he still has his dignity. He deserves no less.

I, and probably most of you, have reached that stage in my life when some very heartbreaking goodbyes are just around the corner. For some of you, it is perhaps a corner on which you've already stood. It is that time in our lives when we are holding doors open for our Dads, out of necessity, as well as respect. When we listen to our Mother's stories for the second time, so grateful they are still here to tell them. It is a time when we have already sat solemnly in a dimly lit church, while our precious friend or maybe even our spouse cried unabashedly as their Mother's or their Father's favorite hymn is sung. It is a time when you have known and loved too many people, not to have felt the heartbreak of a loss due to disease or a senseless tragedy.

My acceptance of this still-miraculous circle of life makes me take a very long and a very hard look at my present. What can I do today that will glorify my faith and satisfy my soul? What are my strengths and more importantly, what are my weaknesses? When will I learn, at last, that the greatest gifts you can give someone are love and acceptance? When will I learn these are also the greatest gifts you can give yourself?

Epilogue: For many of us, this is a time when we know the words of a song from thirty years ago better than the songs that they play today. You go to a concert and look at a once-hip rock group and think to yourself, "My God they look old, but wow, can they still play or what?" Maybe all of us just want to know that we have "played our music" well and that our music has made someone smile!

The Nutrient Imposters

My epiphany for the new millennium came late inspired by the closest thing I'll ever come to having a Marcus Welby, M.D. in my life! By the by, if you are younger than thirty you'll need to know that Dr. Welby was a beloved TV character from the early 70's.

My Dr. Welby's name is Dr. Bill. He is kind and good and although he doesn't make house calls, he truly cares.

"Your body wants food for one reason and one reason only", he explained matter-of-factly. "It wants nutrients. And if you're eating junk food with no nutritional substance, you'll be hungry all the time".

As he was speaking, it was as though a bright light was illuminating the dark corners of my mind...while visions of nutrient-free foods such as Hershey bars, ice cream and chips were still dancing in my head.

When I am hungry, I don't cut up fresh fruit and sit down at the table without any distractions and eat slowly. When I'm "starving", I can't make myself reach for the celery, raw carrots or other fresh veggies. When I am ravenous, I don't look inside my refrigerator or cupboard looking for nutrients.

Quite simply, when I am famished, I am in search of the foods that please me -- chocolate, sugar and salt. Although I've never bothered looking up it up, I have a funny feeling these are nutrient-free food groups.

Who needs vitamins and minerals, when you can run off caffeine and a jolt of glucose surging through your veins? I've struggled with weight my entire life. I have counted, tracked and recorded billions of calories, carbohydrates, and proteins. I have attended hundreds of meetings, seminars and sessions, not to mention the hours logged discussing weight with my girlfriends.

I've always thought I could open up a weight clinic, if it weren't for the whole credibility issue. I have done diets including grapefruit and steaks, ice cream and double-secret cabbage soup. *I've done all of this*...**and still have two-thirds of a closet I can't go near!**

When feeling really desperate, I have had my body mummified in an herbal wrap. It promised to take several inches from my waistline. What it "took away" was the last two glasses of water I had drunk and sixty bucks from my wallet. I have always steered away from undergarment body contour and controllers, fearing I won't recognize myself when I strip down at night. I feel the same way about wearing too much make-up.

Deprivation has never worked for me. So, per my epiphany; I am going to start a new food group called "The Imposters". It will be comprised of all the foods that give me a temporary high, but leave me unsatisfied at the end of the day. I am going to snub this group, as I would any other person or entity I felt was trying to trick me.

Epilogue: I would never waste an epiphany on something as mundane as food. The truth is I have spent a lot of time, money and energy trying to fill my life and myself up with activities and acquisitions that have no real substance.

If my food and my life are going to have value, I need to understand what really gives me strength and joy? **And all these years I thought it was chocolate!**

The Spaghetti Supper

More than twenty years ago, I held what I still refer to today as "The $500 spaghetti supper for 12."

No, I didn't import the spaghetti from Italy! But, I did drive up the price per person by destroying the table on which the supper was served. Did you know, if you place a very hot whatever on a table, moisture seeps through and "blushes" the finish?

It leaves this very pronounced white spot, which no known wood polisher or cleaner can remove. Here's the truly mortifying part of this story: the table, the house…none of it belonged to me! Had it been mine I would have simply hidden the marks with a tablecloth for the rest of its life. The table (and the house where the supper was served) belonged to my sweet friend Cheryl so needless to say I paid to have the top refinished. The unanticipated expenditure represented about five percent of my annual income at the time so you would think it was a lesson I would never forget. I thought wrong.

Flash forward to the Saturday before Easter this year. We had invited my husband Hugh's grandmother, aunts and uncles for a pre-holiday celebration. Several months ago, I was given a recipe for chicken enchilada soup. It has become my one-and-only featured food for company. A featured food item is the one dish, a) You feel confident about and, b) You can actually prepare before guests arrive at your home. For my Mother, it is King Ranch chicken. For many others, it is lasagna.

Because we don't have service for 12, I resorted to the three D's of entertaining - durable, decorative and most importantly, disposable. I had these cute little wicker paper plate holders, Easter napkins and plates and some pretty nifty little soup holders. The featured food went over brilliantly. The party went just fine. Our guests left full and happy.

Imagine my remorse when I took the tablecloth off, only to discover twelve not-so-small white circles on our dining room table.

Flashbacks to the spaghetti supper made me weak in the knees. I called my Mother who, as she tends to do felt my pain.. She was racking her brain, trying to think of any household hint she had ever heard to remedy my woes. This was, of course, after she asked me why I didn't have a pad on my table? Thanks mom!

She then came up with something she'd read, about water stains coming up with a mixture of mayonnaise and ashes. This sounded like some witch's concoction so I asked her if I needed to dance naked around the table and throw a pig's ear over my left shoulder, while I applied the bizarre mixture.

I couldn't bring myself to even look at the table for days, but yesterday I finally got up the courage to mix up my potion. Finding ashes was not a problem, because we have *"that nasty habit"*, but it was very strange stirring them into a bowl with the mayo. I then took a spatula and "iced" the tabletop, all the while wanting to chant a spell. I was to leave the eyesore on for twenty-four hours. Then gently rub it into the surface of the table. When Hugh came home, he looked at the table covered with this yucky stuff and just rolled his eyes.

Epilogue: The mayo and ashes trick did not work on the white spots. The rest of the table looks great. It added luster to the finish, which makes sense in some weird way. I think I recall putting mayonnaise on my hair when I was a teen as well, to get the same effect. I have learned my lesson again. **I will be retiring my featured food for something I can serve for less than $500! I guess this was close enough to Easter to call it what it was...the last supper.**

The Annual Turkey Crap Shoot

When I wake up on Thanksgiving, my mouth starts to water. Not for my own turkey but for my Mom's turkey and dressing. A feast I haven't even tried to replicate in the twenty plus years I've missed sharing this meal with her. It takes me a few minutes to wake up fully and realize that I will be eating my own turkey. **The hunger salivation then turns to cold sweats!**

What I've discovered during my painful turkey past is, the terms moist and actually cooked are mutually exclusive. I've tried oven bags, foil, roasting pans and naked birds coated in butter. Each technique has yielded the same dry, flaky white meat. Thus, I have come up with my own name for this holiday---*The Annual Turkey Crap Shoot*. This bird has defeated me for several years running. This year, this time, I was determined to beat the odds.

What I have long admired about all mothers and grandmothers in the universe is---they can cook eight different items at eight different temperatures and with different techniques and have them all come out cooked and hot at the same time. I make stuffing from a box and yet somehow even it is cold before I am able to heat up the canned green beans. Even with my short cuts, I still have to call my Mother a dozen times, so she can lend moral support as I destroy yet another thirty dollar fowl.

This year, I decided to hedge my bet by buying a hefty turkey breast and cooking it in my crock-pot. "Not even I can dry out a turkey that is sitting in water", I foolishly boasted to myself. Six hours later, I was poking the meat thermometer into this stupid bird, noting it looked so unlike a turkey should, with its' pale yellow skin and pinkish white meat. "Ah-hah, I will take the turkey from the water, coat it in butter and stick it in the oven".

I learned that the "you can't judge a book by its' cover" also applies to turkey, as the skin was a succulent golden brown and the white meat was as it always has been---dry and flaky. As always, I had to skip the carving ritual as then my guests could see there were no juices flowing from the bird. I have developed my own tradition, which is to peel the meat off in dry clumps, dump a ton of gravy on it and pray that no one is the wiser.

I was demoralized and close to tears, so I called my Mom. She told me a turkey crapshoot tale that made me smile. Mom began her day by preheating the oven at nine AM. Prompted by a burning smell, she rescued three perfectly empty and now scorching cookie sheets from the oven at approximately 9:30 AM. At the same time, she popped her bird into the oven, to begin the six-hour wait. At noon, prompted by no smell at all this time, she checked on the turkey only to find the oven and the bird were stone cold. She had apparently turned the oven off completely when she removed her twice-done cookie sheets! She then had to do the unimaginable, for a woman who never misses a dinner deadline. Which is to call her son, Jeff (my brother), to postpone the feast until five o'clock.

Epilogue: Jeff and his family happily adjusted their arrival time, as he knows what I am just now learning---**There are still things in this life that are worth waiting for!**

Ever-Ready Betty

It began as just girl talk in my sister, Diane's, kitchen over the 4th of July. *Why don't we, the sisters, take Mom on an all-girl vacation?* If anyone's mom was owed a few days of frolic and fun for all she had done for her daughters, it was our Mom. We began brainstorming on potential destinations that would not meet with husband-and-children protest. Obviously, any type of amusement park or far away exotic place was out of the question. My nephew, Paul, strolled into the kitchen on the tail end of our discussion. Since we hadn't come up with a city so far, I asked him, "Paul, where could your Mom, Grandma, Aunt Diane and I go, where WE could have fun with no husbands or children? Paul, a high school senior typically bored with anything having to do with his Mom and her sisters, actually pondered my question. After several moments, he came up with an idea that made perfect sense, since he didn't know we were talking about a road trip. *"Cloth World"*, he replied. We laughed! Good answer Paul but not even we could enjoy a fabric store for a full three days!

We eventually settled on New York City, based on, a) unparalleled shopping opportunities and b) a beautiful downtown apartment to stay in compliments of my friend Monica. The money we would save on lodging provided us with a bigger budget to blow on shopping and entertainment. We began negotiating dates for our girls-only get-away via E-mail. It was no small feat, coming up with three days in which four women with five children, four husbands, and three jobs could break away the same time. It was good fortunate that, at the time we booked our flights, I had no idea I would be moving three weeks later proving for the hundredth time that ignorance is bliss.

Somewhere between booking the flights, packing up the house and actually leaving for the trip, I managed to come down with what my doctor kept telling me was walking pneumonia. I believe the correct term is 'selective listening' as I chose to cling to the word walking versus pneumonia as I packed my suitcase and headed for the airport.

Adhering to the mantra of modern living: 'If you can't cure it, mask it!' I was able to take enough medicine to subdue that pesky diagnosis for three days.

There is no place in the world like New York City and we had a great time! We saw a show on Broadway, had drinks at the Rainbow Room and took in the Christmas splendor at Rockefeller Center. We talked, we ate and we shopped! We even spent hours at Saks Fifth Avenue crammed into one dressing room, watching sister Diane try on beautiful gowns for her holiday party. When she found the one that made her look like a Princess, it was more gratifying than if it was our own.

Epilogue: I would tell you that we kept the pace slow for our mother's sake but the truth was that *she slowed down for us!* On the flight home, I was, as always, lulled to sleep by the humming of the plane engines. I awoke about an hour later, still tired and groggy. I looked across the aisle to see my two sisters sound asleep, our "senior Mom" wide awake, knitting something and chatting with the woman next to her. All I could think of was the 'Eveready battery bunny'...*SHE'S STILL GOING!* It made me tired just watching her so I fell back asleep.

I'm not certain we made the best travel companions, but these three women are the most beloved women in my life. I'd do it all again in a New York minute.

The Pig & The Hound

We are leaving for our annual Christmas pilgrimage in only four days. There is much life to be squeezed in prior to our departure so I find myself typing this column at midnight on Sunday. It seems that everyone is trying to manage their reality with more humanity than most years, trying to leave room for the miracles of the season to take place. We are were so busy moving when we got home from Texas last year, I never shared the tale of *The Night the Pig Lay Down with the Hound.*

My Mom and her husband, Jay, live in a typical Texas neighborhood, which sits on a golf course backing on a wooded area. Like most suburbanites, they spend a lot of time and energy grooming the yard and take great pride in their garden beds. Imagine my Mother's face one morning when she woke up to find all her garden beds had been foraged by some animal? She could tell at once the extensive rooting was not the work of a wild dog or a mere rodent. These tunnels of dirt had been dug by something much more menacing. So she set out to apprehend the culprit.

It was several weeks later before she saw with her own eyes the cause of all this havoc in their neighborhood. It seems somehow a wild pig had survived the urbanization and came out of his small forest to find food in more fertile ground. Not only was the wild pig cavorting about the neighborhood at night destroying garden beds, he had taken up company with her next-door-neighbor's dog. An unlikely, but very real; "dynamic duo."

She passed the story onto me. In the rush of all the goings-on, I never relayed the hilarious discovery to husband Hugh, who then became the next good story.

'Twas two nights before Christmas and all through the house, not a creature was stirring except husband, Hugh. He had been sleeping restlessly so he went outside in the middle of the night to smoke. Then what to his wondering eyes did appear, but a wild pig running -- with a dog at his heels. He spoke not a word but flew straight to the house, to wake up his wife with a very loud shout. "Honey, wake up, I think I've lost my mind!" I responded as I would to any piece of news shouted at me at four in the morning. "Huh?" He is still breathing heavily, but continues, "I was just outside and I swear that I saw a wild pig in your Mom's driveway! And he was with a dog!"

Now I was awake and giggling hysterically, which was met with a very grim look from the still-shaken Hugh. I finally stopped laughing long enough to explain that he was quite sane. Yes, the neighborhood was home to a snorting wild pig. Had I not told him this? Hmmm, could have sworn that I told him! I waited until he was asleep and breathing normally before I turned off the light, smiled to myself and fell sound asleep.

Epilogue: Hugh and I are very different. The way I see it is, if a dog and a pig can commingle peacefully, then so can we.

Project Management

Dad and his wife Suzie will be seeing our home for the first time in just four weeks! Since the term "honey-do list" seems so passé, I have adapted this colloquialism to the new millennium by calling it a "home project calendar".

Although husband Hugh is a computer kind of guy himself, he was not thrilled to receive my wish list on a time line generated by a very nifty calendar program on our PC. You can enter each project and then this miracle program can sort by start date, due date, responsible party and hours necessary to complete the task. It is, in short, a husband's worst nightmare because, in nine out of ten cases, the husband is the 'responsible party.' I don't have an official title in this program, but if I were forced to choose one, I suppose it would be Project Coordinator. I ran this title by husband Hugh. It was met with a grimace. I can't imagine why?

I like being Project Coordinator, what wife wouldn't? Like many couples we have issues in our marriage that evolve around how we assign priorities. Hugh believes balancing our checkbook is more important than hanging the knick-knack shelf in our bedroom. I respectfully disagree. Clearly, having this very cute knick-knack shelf lying on the floor next to our bed does not eat at the very core of his very being, as it does me!

Each day, my project list and me must compete against the demands of Hugh's everyday responsibilities. We often lose. My Dad has unwittingly become the perfect foil in this battle, as he was handyman extraordinaire. As an engineer by trade, he could build or repair just about anything around our house. In fact, he built our first home! So, as you can see, it is a tough act for any son-in-law to follow. Thankfully, he retired from his own roof repair projects about ten years ago after much "discussion" with his wife, Suzie, and his children. As a handy guy, his motto for years was…"Nobody does it better."

I suppose it is destined to be that all daughters of handy fathers grow up to be "project managers." Especially when I married an engineer myself. Hugh can tackle just about any job around our house that he chooses to. His talents have not gone unnoticed by me. This has become his cross to bear. Here's the tricky part. My father-in-law, Tom, is an integral part of this project calendar. As a retired commercial plumbing foreman, he brings very integral skills to this plan. Our mission is to install electrical outlets and a bathroom in the basement. That's all! I showed Tom the time line for his approval. Like his son, he was not very excited about seeing my schedule for him in print.

Epilogue: While Hugh and his Dad do not see eye to eye on all things, on this they have agreed. They are going to fire me…if I show them the stupid project calendar one more time. Although they have not said so out loud, I know that in their minds I have been demoted from management to water "boy" for this project. They claim they can get it done together without me. *I wonder if they realize that this was the plan all along?*

The 'Phone Zone'

If I want to get my husband's full attention, I need only pick up a phone.

While I have not completely tested this theory, I probably wouldn't even have to actually make a call. It seems to be the act of only holding the phone that captures his attention. I recognize I am only one of millions of women searching for phone freedom.

I don't know what it is. As soon as I am talking to a third party, suddenly Hugh wants to be involved in the conversation. Here's a "for instance". We will both be sitting downstairs, me flipping through a magazine, him watching a ballgame. I have what I consider to be an important news flash. I attempt to interrupt him, "Honey, did I tell you I have an appointment in Alabama next Tuesday?" Hugh's reply, "Uhuh." "Uhuh" translates in our house to "No and I didn't really hear you just now either---I am making this guttural sound to acknowledge I saw your lips move, with the hope you will not provide me with any more detail at this time!"

Same scenario, five minutes later. The phone rings, it is my girlfriend, Alison. I move into the kitchen with the cordless phone, out of Hugh's earshot. We are catching up in general. At some point, I relay to Alison the same information I tried to tell Hugh, "I am going to Alabama next Tuesday." Suddenly, the husband- eavesdropping-antennae goes up and he shouts from the den, "Honey, you didn't tell me you were going out of town next week!" He has now officially tuned into our conversation. If I choose to remain on the phone, I would be having a three-way conversation from this moment forward. Some of the husband-phone interloping techniques include, "Tell Alison I said 'Hi'", or "Did you tell Alison about whatever?" or, my personal favorite, "Let me speak to her a minute?" Or, if he is not in the mood to participate but still wants to intervene, the nebulous question routine begins. "Honey, where is the remote control?" "Do you know where my tennis shoes are?"

I have contended with the phone freedom issue long before I was ever married. For years as a single woman with married friends, I would be stunned that I could call them and five minutes into the conversation, the tone and tenor of their voices would change. I suspected then what I can confirm now...their husband had entered the "phone zone." *Do they think we are talking about them? Please!*

I have but one real place of phone freedom now, which is my cell phone while driving alone. Yesterday I drove to Greenville, SC and spent the entire trip burning up my free minutes. People warn you that cell phones can be recorded and that random strangers can, and do, pick up your signal and use it for themselves. I don't care! I would ten times rather have a stranger listening in than my own husband. Why? Because these outsiders don't want to chime in, that's why. We can talk freely about whatever silly or serious subject we want to, in peace.

Epilogue: I don't know why men are so possessive, when it comes to their mates being on the phone. *I do know that this male tendency is causing me to spend all of my slush fund on my cell phone bill!*

Rocky Mountain High

Top three questions you don't want to hear from your driver as you descend Trail Ridge Road, the highest paved road in America: **"Can you smell that? Does that smell like burning rubber to you? Do you think my brakes are OK?"** Hugh was in the back seat of the SUV, gazing out the rolled down window. The thin mountain air was giving him a "Rocky Mountain High", robbing him of his ability to hear. He was blissfully unaware of the mortifying Q&A going on in the front seat between our tour guide (and dear friend), Joyce, and myself. I was clutching my door as though this could save me should we plummet ten thousand feet, while Joyce tapped the brakes all the way down the mountain. She seemed not to be overly concerned for our safety. She was pointing out particular mountains by name and elevations, none of which I recall. I watched amazed as Joyce and Hugh took in the splendor, while I asked myself the question I was raised to ask when faced with a potential trip to the hospital…"Am I wearing decent underwear?!"

Neither Hugh nor I had ever been to Colorado. We flew out there last weekend for our last holiday of the summer. It was everything we knew it would be, as the Rocky Mountains are breathtaking. Hailing from a city, where the highest peak is a freeway ramp, these mountains struck me as no less than nature's masterpiece. It's a real shame that, due to the change in altitude, all we really wanted to do was sleep.

We did manage to squeeze in some sightseeing in between naps. We even took a half-a-hike. All over Boulder and the rest of Colorado, there are people who can trek up these trails with ease! What I found even more amazing was they could actually speak while they hike! I felt like I needed an oxygen tank while just walking on level ground.

Since long hikes were not an option for us, sweet Joyce drove us around, hoping to find some wildlife for we city folk to enjoy. We saw prairie dog colonies galore. We did finally spot the rear ends of some elk in the woods. Like every other tourist, I made her stop the car, so that I could take some classic U.F.O. (Unidentifiable Foreign Objects) pictures.

U.F.O.'s are photos taken by an amateur photographer of something, in the distance that no one, not even the person taking the photo, can identify once the film has been developed.

My film is ready to be picked up. I know that my friends and family will love shuffling through stacks of photos with me. As if being handed a stack a pictures isn't bad enough, all U.F.O. pictures require narration. "Can you see that blurry brown spot in the woods? That's an elk". Sadly, there will come a point in my life when even I won't recall that the brown spot is an elk's behind!

Epilogue: I've never been what some refer to as a "granola nut". I don't litter, but that's probably because the television commercial from the sixties with the Native American Indian in the canoe really stuck. Rather than try to teach environmental awareness from a text, I now believe that everyone should just go to Colorado. *Because once you stand at the foot of these majestic mountains, there is no question in your mind as to who's the boss...It's definitely not us!*

It's Not Easy, Being Green

I have a long-standing boycott against most women's magazines because a) I don't know any women who look like these cover "girls" and b) I've taken all the sex and romance compatibility 'tests' that I am willing to take in one lifetime. How about the men take a "How to Please Your Mate' survey for a change! Anyway, since there is not much else to do at a hair salon, I use my time there for personal reflection. I don't reflect too deeply, as it's hard to get serious while feeling like a character from Star Trek. I look around at the other aluminum-filled heads, noting all of us look like we could contact the mother ship by just nodding our heads.

Those of us who have our hair professionally colored have either, A) always had the means to do so, or B) done something tragic to our own hair once upon a time. I fall into category B, as I spent ten months of my life as the poster child for the song, "It's Not Easy Being Green".

Like many women my age, I lived through the Sun-In era of orange streaks surrounding our bangs and face. So enchanted with our duo-tone look, we migrated to brush-on highlights that resembled Cruella DeVille's style. Neither of these techniques would do when we graduated from high school, as we were in search of a more sophisticated frosted look. This is when we discovered the now infamous self-frosting caps. As a society we reject torture…yet as women, we embrace self-inflicted pain for the sake of better hair.

I can recall sitting for hours with an extremely tight-fitting rubber cap on my head, while a "friend" jabbed my scalp with a hook, pulling long hair through small holes. On one such occasion, we left the cap on too long and took every ounce of pigment out of my then dishwater-blonde hair. The Edgar Winter look was not becoming to me. So I did what any collegiate on a two hundred dollar-a-month budget would do. I went to the grocery store for a remedy. Five hours and four boxes of hair dye later, I had avocado green hair. I had no choice but to call in reinforcements, so I dialed my Mother collect.

I sobbed while I told her my tale of woe, but that didn't relieve the tension by much. She told me to come home. The two expensive and tedious days to follow were not amongst our finest days together. The color specialist tried every trick available, yet my hair simply changed shades of green. Here are seven words no woman wants to hear about her hair...for any reason. *"It will just have to grow out!"*

Growing out a bad hair dye job or a bad perm is the ultimate example of something beyond our control. We have, in a small way, challenged Mother Nature. No bobby pin, no head ban, no hat can hide the fact your hair has two distinctly different colors (or textures). You simply must accept the fact your hair looks horrible. You endure the next several months by sharing your hair story with any person unfortunate enough to stand next to you for longer than ten seconds.

Epilogue: This true tale is why I am a card carrying member of the "pay now or pay later hair club for women." When Hugh and I were trying to cut back our expenses, I defended my right to professional hair care with vigor. I pointed out that cable TV cost about the same ...perhaps we should consider that a line item veto. *Have Georgia Tech football on the cutting room floor?* **I didn't think so!**

Hoarding

A couple of years back; I broke open my piggy band to give husband, Hugh, a Mont Blanc pen & pencil set. He loved them. He spent at least an hour, writing innocuous notes to test them out and to revel in his fine writing instruments. Much as this gift was a winner, *I have not seen the pen or pencil since that day!*

Here's Hugh's big secret -- he has a pen and pencil fetish. Like an eccentric collector of priceless paintings, he hides them away for only his pleasure. When I am presented with a gift carrying any type of brand name stature, I display it...like any normal person would. I mean really, what's the point in owning a Coach purse, if you're going to keep it in your closet?

Hugh is not a snob. He is an equal opportunity hoarder. His pen fetish extends to cheap-but-treasured pens as well. If I ask him to "Hand me a pen please", he has to look through his stash to locate a writing instrument he is willing to let go of... if only for a minute. He'll hand me some topless pen with barely enough ink left to sign my name...and then quickly look away, so he can't see my glare!

This pen thing is so contrary to how Hugh is with everything else, it just crawls right under my skin. He doesn't care I've taken possession of his Mother's diamond tennis bracelet. But I better not be caught with his Dr. Grip mechanical pencil! What is that about?

It must be a gender issue, since I witnessed this same hoarding behavior this weekend with our dog, Champ. "Molly", my father-in-laws new dog by marriage, came to stay with us for a few days, while he and his new bride were on their honeymoon. It was a very gratifying experience meeting a pooch more spoiled than our own. We loved having her around. Champ, having been raised as an only doggie, does not work and play well with others. Most notably, he does not share -- a very unattractive characteristic in any mammal.

Miss Molly made the grave mistake of locating an old bone, hidden months ago underneath the guest bed. Although Champ had not chewed on this particular treat in months, he became quite jealous. Suddenly, our aging Mr. Champ was a virile pup again, aggressing on poor Molly like she had attempted to rob him of his family jewels. Now he was paranoid, so his little fit didn't stop there. Champ then proceeded to scour the entire house for any bone which might be at risk of being stolen. He brought them all back to my office. He put four bones in a pile and stood watch over them the rest of the time, only leaving for food and bathroom breaks. *Like father, like son!*

Epilogue: Here's the upside to this whole pen obsession. If I need Hugh's help running errands, I just have to mention "office supply store" and he is on board.

He'd be so embarrassed if he knew I disclosed how long he is able to entertain himself on the pen aisle!! I know I should count my blessings. The average price of a pen is $3 and I can't think of one thing I covet that cost less than a hundred.

"Mom" School

Our dear friends, Rob and Alison, have been blessed by the arrival of their son, Matthew Robert. Alison is adjusting to sleep deprivation. Rob is adjusting to having a new man in the house. I am adjusting to the changes in a friendship that occur anytime there is a major lifestyle transformation. Since change is the only thing we can count on, my philosophy has always been, "embrace with enthusiasm the new boyfriend ... husband...child" of your close friends. This is much easier to do with a sweet baby, than a man, who is now taking up all of your now estranged friend's time.

I sit in her living room, amazed by the gear that comes with this infant child. Where husband, Hugh, has one recliner -- infant Matt has six. He has his choice of one which bounces, one that glides, one to swing in, one stationary which plays music, one that transforms into a car seat *and one that apparently can do all of the above!* Each time I visit their home, Matthew Robert looks more and more like a little boy. Each time I visit, there is yet another infant educational toy either fully assembled or in the staging area, which used to be their living room.

Yesterday it was a Discovery Farm Entertainment Center. Made of baby-proof plastic with bold primary colors, this moving, noisemaking, attention grabber, will keep Matt busy for literally *moments* at a time. Alison's fantasy and every mom's fantasy is -- the Discovery Farm will keep their child busy long enough for them to take a shower alone. I can assure you, in the early sixties, my discovery farm was simply anything I could reach from inside my playpen.

I have never gone to "Mom School"! So I had no idea what an ordeal it was, just to run a simple errand. It took us a mere thirty minutes to collect everything necessary for any and every eventuality. Although children don't come with instructions, all this equipment surely must. Having never read the manuals, I am zero help in putting stuff together, or, most importantly, collapsing any of the above aforementioned baby equipment.

I ended up breaking a sweat in the parking lot of Babies R Us. Still I couldn't find the magic button that makes that dang stroller collapse. I have since wrestled a baby jogger and a playpen. In both cases, my opponent was the clear victor. Finding the release button on the car seat? Not going to happen! Matt cried, I panicked and Mom had to come to the rescue. I don't think poor Alison knew who to comfort first.

So many gizmos, so little time. There is the wiper warmer, the feeding system (AKA bottle), the baby monitors, ear thermometers, and the designer snuggy. My personal favorite is the "Can't-live-without Diaper Genie". I am convinced this product was designed and named by a Mom somewhere, whispering to herself, "If I had one wish, it would be to have a place for these dirty diapers!" Poof, the Diaper Genie was conceived. *Bet she wishes now she had wished for a nanny to take the night shift instead!*

Epilogue: For everything that has changed, the important things remain the same. Matthew Robert is hugged and loved by Rob and Alison...in the same way all good parents have loved their children since the beginning of time.

Matt, I may not be able to collapse your stroller, but I want to be part of your life. Let's make a date for when you start to eat sand in the sandbox. *I got a A+ in sand-eating!*

Pulling an All-Nighter

Do you remember when we were twenty years old and could function on three hours of sleep? *These infamous "all-nighters" were primarily devoted to learning a semester of college in twelve hours!*

A study method, I understand, which has a widespread following even today. We would drink coffee; eat pizza and study until almost dawn. We would then crash for three hours, shower and show up to take the final exam at 10 AM.

I never did well on those exams, but that had nothing to do with my lack of sleep and everything to do with me overestimating my own IQ. I occasionally allowed myself to wonder if my parents had been telling me the truth, when they said my older siblings actually did their homework in college. I didn't let this unsettling thought disrupt my thinking for too long.

The amazing part of this story is, after the exam was over, I could continue all day in high gear. My young mind was still alert and my body rested enough to perform high-level functions, such as eating, walking, and gossiping.

Flash forward 25 years. Hugh and I went to bed last night at 11:00 PM, so w e could get up at 4:30 AM for Easter Sunrise Service. We drank enough coffee to stay awake for the drive down to our church, to be able to actually absorb the message delivered by our beloved minister and friend, Ellen, and for the drive back home. We are now delirious.

Maybe it is the cumulative effect of all we have going on in our lives but five hours of sleep just isn't enough anymore. I had big plans for getting another room packed in-between church and lunch at Hugh's Dad's house. **Clearly a fantasy!** My goal instead is to try to finish my column, without nodding off to sleep and drooling on my keyboard.

So here we sit on the single most important day of our Christian faith. What are we?...We are *crabby!* It doesn't really matter if you are four years old or 44 years old. If you don't get the sleep your body needs, it will let you know. Since biologically speaking I am an adult, I can't give in to my basic instinct to rub my eyes and burst out in tears. I can't just run around the house screaming until I crash on the floor somewhere. I have to be grown-up enough to realize I need a nap, without anyone telling me so.

Hugh didn't fight the urge to sleep like I did. He and our dog, Champ, cuddled up in bed snoozing, while I was still pretending I was twenty years old. I went into the bathroom to splash water on my face and caught myself scowling, for no reason at all. Out of fear I might encounter someone else in my short-tempered state, I finally poured myself into bed. Our family nap lasted over two hours. When we awoke we were all more humane.

Epilogue: When I watch the news, listening to the hard-to-bear accounts of road rage, crimes of passion and war, I wonder if the entire world is suffering from sleep deprivation. Maybe we have all gotten so busy and so industrious, we don't give our minds, our bodies and our souls the rest they so desperately need.

Maybe mankind needs a nice long nap to make the world a better place!

Yard Envy

In my world, "the grass is literally always greener on the other side of the street" since all of our neighbors have sprinkler systems. While we've been schlepping one hundred foot hoses around in a feeble attempt to save our fescue lawn, the Bermuda grass in the lawns surrounding us has remained green and luscious. I am suffering from *yard envy*.

Hugh and I stood on our back deck like Myrtle the Turtles, "king and queen of all we survey". We realized this big, brown patch of fescue was indeed ours to fix. It is easy to see things for what they really are after a drought or "dry spell". I mean this both literally and figuratively. When we bought our house, we had visions of our half-acre side lot being the envy of all of our neighbors with a vast blanket of emerald green grass. Now, from our aerial view, it looked like a patchwork quilt gone awry. We had the barely living fescue, dead fescue, patches of Bermuda grass, as well as the big naked spots of red Georgia clay, where nothing was growing but rocks and small chunks of concrete.

At least we thought the concrete chunks were small! As we couldn't afford to get the whole yard graded and start anew, we hired reinforcements to unearth the mess left behind by the construction workers buried just beneath the surface. Hugh wanted to wait until we had more time. I, of course, assured him that it would only take half a day and I'll help! Come to find out, the little bits of concrete we could see were just the tip of the iceberg. I resigned my helper position, when I saw them struggle with the first three-foot block of rock. I tried to make myself useful as the water girl. Four men, ten hours, three pick axes and two broken shovels later, we had a five-foot mountain of concrete and a full-blown tree in the middle of our yard. By the end of this grueling project, the men had lost ten pounds and all the water in the world couldn't drench their thirst. Hugh was not smiling. Even the men we paid were not smiling. OK, OK, so maybe my plan was just a tad ambitious!

The unhappy crew was not up for a second day of fun. So we disposed of our buried treasure and put landscape flags around the big holes. It won't surprise you to learn I was put in charge of filling the holes with dirt---since I had insisted this was an easy project. This only took me the better part of a Sunday. Now our "quilt" included patches of deep brown topsoil, as well. If our poor yard could have blushed from embarrassment, it surely would have.

The amazing thing about yard revival efforts is every amateur on your block and every paid professional has their own methodology for raising a yard from the dead. Hugh and I were lost in the maze of ways to aerate, fertilize, re-seed, and grade our pitiful piece of the American dream.

Epilogue: In the end, we choose the most risky and most expensive option because I believed it to be the quickest--- we laid down sod. My yard envy has netted me fun-filled mornings with those stupid hoses, attempting to keep the sod alive. I thought I had learned that envy of any kind---for any reason---never leads to anything good. One hour each morning I have the opportunity to learn this lesson again, **THE HARD WAY!**

Spring Break

For "Spring Break", Sister Diane and her family are jetting off to Greece. Brother Jeff and his family are taking off for Aruba. Hugh and I are going to our back yard. I don't normally covet my siblings' good fortunes. But I found myself feeling a little green over their travels. In these pure, unadulterated and undeserved moments of self-pity, I did what many children do - - *I called my Mother!*

She listened to me whine for a while, then she explained she and Jay would be shuttling each other back and forth to the medical center for their "Spring Break". Suddenly our backyard started looking *really* good!

The irony is, until I had one, a yard was something else I coveted. I imagined myself in a big straw hat, cutting beautiful blooms out of my garden, located just behind my white picket fence. We live in a brand new house - - there is not a bloom in sight. In fact, I'm just praying the bushes out front, which look perfectly dead, are going to do something when the weather gets nicer. Right now, they are unidentifiable twigs in the dirt. Even my friends, who know shrubbery can't identify a literal 'stick-in-the-mud!'

Gardening and lawn care...yet another area of seduction for the new homeowner/would-be gardener. Perhaps I tipped my hand at the nursery, when I asked what "deciduous" meant. This woman knew she had found a novice. So she wisely followed me around her shop for the next hour. I purchased several climbing vines, a trellis, a few bulbs, and a lot of dirt. "Good dirt", I'm told. It has made me wonder? *What is wrong with me* that I purchase large quantities of readily available natural resources such as dirt and water?

Before I left the nursery, my new garden mentor handed me well over twenty brochures, on such topics as hummingbird gardens, vegetable growing and soil treatments. I was on overload. I am a woman who has gardened in a twelve-inch ceramic pot for twenty-plus years. My "just add water" mentality was not going to see me through this chore.

My truckload and me arrived home, just in time to wake Husband Hugh up from his nap. He got to help me unload the 10 forty-pound bags of good dirt. He was so excited! That same day, I filed away my many brochures for a rainy day. Since we've had several of those lately, I now know what deciduous means. That dead-looking twig in my front yard is a deciduous something. I'm not sure I care how gorgeous a plant gets in the spring if it spends nine months looking like my house plants look all year.

Epilogue: Because Hugh and I don't have children of our own, it was merely a coincidence I chose Spring Break to embark on my new obsession. Spring Break hasn't held any meaning for me since 1981 when I took my scholarship money and flew to Cancun, Mexico.

I don't know why I took notice of it this year or why I would be envious of my siblings' good fortune. A very wise woman once told me, true peace is "wanting what you already have." *I think I will adjust my attitude...buy a big straw hat and plant my garden...in peace!*

Think System

I'm utilizing Professor Harold Hill's "Think System", made famous in *The Music Man*, to pack up our house. There is no physical exertion in the "Think System". *You simply concentrate very hard on the task at hand and...miraculously you are an accomplished musician, or, in my case...a ready-to-move homeowner!*

Husband Hugh is starting to get nervous. Frankly, so am I. We are moving in less than one month. There is not one box actually packed. However, I have *thought* about where the furniture will be placed. I have *thought* about which items we need to sell. I have *thought* a great deal about how to pack. Just yesterday, I packed inside my head for over three hours. It was exhausting. The day before, I thought about pricing everything for the big moving sale. I had to take a nap afterwards. Today, I plan to think through which kitchen items to store and which items to take with us. I hope I'm not too tired tonight to start thinking about clearing the garage.

I have been daunted by the challenge before me. I know, in order to accomplish my task, I must separate fantasy from reality, fact from fiction, the real from the imaginary. I hate that! It is so much nicer to live in the world inside my head...where everything is possible and all endings are happy ones...just like in all the great musicals.

For instance, I will only have room in our new place for one clothing size. Which size, pray tell, shall I take? Do I take the comfortable size I can actually sit down in, without experiencing stomach pain? Do I take the size that zips, but just barely and only in a reclining position? Or shall I bring along the size that used–to-be-me, never leave our apartment, to have only my rich fantasy life as my social interaction?

I then start thinking about our kitchen, which is simply more fertile ground for my fanciful flights. Do I pack the food processor we got as a wedding gift four years ago, which I have never used? I have prepared a dozen meals in my mind's eye, requiring hours of chopping and grinding and peeling. How can I prepare these delectable feasts, without my food processor? Should I take the garbage sack filled with crumpled white linen napkins to use at my imaginary banquets, those I have meticulously ironed and folded in my dreams? The question before me is so simple, yet the answer seems so complex -- *which world do I truly want to live in?*

Epilogue: Meredith Wilson created Professor Hill circa 1957. He introduced millions of Americans to the excitement of the trombone and to marching bands. My Dad would play *The Music Man* every Sunday morning on the Heathkit Hi-Fi he put together himself. It is no coincidence I chose "Seventy-Six Trombones" as the first song at our wedding reception.

It is no small wonder I can sing almost every word from every well-known musical ever written. And it comes as no surprise I can watch one of these glorious productions for the hundredth time...slipping away to a more simple time. Thank you, Dad! The world can get a little tough sometimes. *The music you taught me to love all those years ago can still take my blues away, even in the real world!*

White Water Frenzy!

For years I have been missing a vital piece of pop-culture. I think I am the only person who did not see the movie Deliverance in the seventies!

Not only did I miss the movie, I never read a review or spoke to anyone in depth about it. I've believed until this year, it was simply a funny flick about some guys on a rafting trip.

The theme song, "Dueling Banjos", is deceivingly upbeat. So who knew it was a movie that haunts even the actors to this day? What I did miss was the white water rafting mania. I've wanted to take one of these trips for years now.

Yesterday was Hugh's and my second trip of the summer and it was an outdoor adventure for sure! In order to tell a tale, one must set the stage.

I will begin with our costumes. In addition to our ratty looking bathing suits, we were sporting river shoes that made Hugh and I look like two giant elves. This basic ensemble is then complimented by a dingy life jacket and, in the case of the Ocoee River, a helmet.

The helmet should have been my first clue that we were in for a very rough ride!

Thankfully, they don't turn novices loose on the rapids by themselves. Our guide was Matt, the Canadian. He was young, very "buff" and very funny. There were seven of us in the boat to begin with. All in all, we were a hearty crew. This is a polite way of saying we probably tipped the scales a little---which caused us to drag bottom, where other boats floated on by.

We "put in" on what was supposed to be a manageable rapid. Within twenty seconds, four out of seven of us were in the river, free-floating. I won't go into detail. Except to say, once you get over the fear of dying, it is just plain embarrassing. All I recall is Matt hoisting me in, while I was crying out Hugh's name.

We recovered from our spill and managed to pass through several rapids without incident, until we came to a very "technical" rapid.

Technical is code for "narrow passing". We found ourselves lodged precariously on a rock, smack dab in the middle of some pretty wicked rapids.

Matt, the guide, had to jump out and try to dislodge his hearty crew from the rock. He disappeared for several long moments under the raft. When he popped up on the other side, he exclaimed, "You're never going to believe what happened! I've lost my shorts!"

So here is Matt, our only chance at survival, trapped naked in the river. Before I even had a chance to process this news flash, one of our fellow rafters, Craig, stands up in the boat and begins taking off his swimsuit to give it to Matt.

Craig had wisely "layered" his clothing that morning, so his desire to live prevailed over his modestly and his pride. At this point, we now have a pretty much naked Craig and a nude guide in our boat. You could hear the howls of laughter echoing off the riverbanks from the other rafters!

Another guide had to abandon his ship to assist in our rescue. One of his crew generously donated her shorts to Craig. Which I was grateful for, since I was sitting right behind him on the raft!

Epilogue: The next time I'm looking for white water adventure, I'm going to a water park with some borrowed children. Where helmets aren't required and **your only fear is running into someone you know while in your bathing suit!**

The Traveler's Twilight Zone

Mind-numbing traffic is more appealing to me than cooling my personal jets, while my plane shuts theirs off and hangs out on the runway. **This is the traveler's 'Twilight Zone'...caught between boarding and takeoff, somewhere on the tarmac!** It is normally an "Act of God", like nasty weather, that lands a plane in the twilight zone. Either way, you aren't getting to where you are going nor are you going where you've been...you are somewhere in between. Since neither God nor his sidekick, "Mother Nature", have ever felt obliged to completely unlock the secrets of weather you are at their mercy.

So you sit. The first hour isn't horrible, as at this point you're still hopeful you are actually going to depart eventually. You wait for the comforting sound of the engines starting up again or the captain's voice over the P.A., telling you you're in line for take-off. Hour Two---Your hope begins to dwindle; you join the silent prayer vigil that the infant two rows up will continue to doze. Hour Three---The anxiety level climbs for business travelers, whose laptop battery is now dead, and parents traveling with small children who at this point totally bored with their array of toys. The captain periodically lets us know he knows nothing, which is more comforting than it should be. Hour four---You could cut the tension with a knife...only, of course, no one has a knife or any pointed object anymore. Smokers (such as myself) are going quietly insane, wondering how many months we'd spend in jail for rushing the crew and deploying the emergency slide, just for *ONE* cigarette.

It was almost 10 PM when, at last, the engines began their powerful rumble. My fellow passengers and I were ecstatic...until we realized we were taxing back to the gate. Apparently the storms had cleared, but now our crew was over their flight time limit. A now very grumpy band of passengers disembarked from the plane to face our gate agent, people trained in hysteria management. These folks make the guards at Buckingham Palace look like amateurs, when it comes to lack of facial expression. There is no emergency, sob story or fit of rage that will make them sweat. I joined the huddled masses and waited my turn in line.

I was eventually re-booked on another airline for the following morning, given absolute assurance my bags would catch up with me at my final destination. Since I am way too much of a control freak to accept that answer, I began my quest to rescue my bags from the system. It was two hours later when I realized the gate agent must have thrown away my envelope with my claim stubs during the ticket switch.

Desperate people do desperate things. I went back to the now deserted gate. I began digging through the trash, looking for my tags. There were a few weary travelers nearby looking at me with some curiosity. The person I really confused was the custodial person waiting nearby. I could see she was torn between calling Security versus "the little white men in their little white coats" as she watched me methodically rummage through all three trashcans.

Epilogue: Under the unspoken "don't ask, don't tell" rule that governs many things best left unsaid, the gate agent for the new airline never questioned how I produced those lost claim tickets. I was reunited with my bags, my husband, my dog and my bed. **The next morning I simply "got up and did it again! Amen."**

Life is a Highway and My Car is Stalled

My life has become a metaphor of a two-lane road with a stalled car in the middle. Things are so backed up now; I can't even tell what's causing the delay.

I do know I never catch up at work...my beloved African children are being completely ignored...I start most conversations with friends and family with, "I'm sorry that I haven't...," I could no longer pass for a true blonde...all meals at our house are served out of a bag or a box. I don't think husband Hugh has noticed this yet thanks to the World Series, but that diversion ends this weekend.

Saturdays can be likened to the intersection on this two-lane highway called life, because everything piles up at this point. All the big and small things I can't get done during the workweek collide in these eight hours of mayhem. I've discovered you can either move through these intersections with no mishaps...or get stuck right in the middle, when the light turns red. For example, I can be somewhat enjoying a manicure when I look at the clock, realizing the dry cleaners are closing right that very minute and my outfit for the evening is now locked securely inside. It's hard to be glad for manicured nails when you're wearing sweatpants to the ball.

And what or who is the stalled car in this analogy? It is, of course, the person or thing beyond my control. It is the customer, who wouldn't buy what I was selling; the Internet connection down for repair; the child with a fever; the husband with a late flight; a run in my last pair of pantyhose. *Some days, it's just my own stalled car!*

I can't tell you how much these roadblocks in life used to torment me. I think it was because I felt singled out; that these things happened simply to ruin my day. I am proud to say, I have since gotten over myself realizing (at last) I'm not the only person stuck on this road. I no longer hang my head out of the window and yell to the person only one car in front of me, "Hey, do you know what's going on up there"? I'm sure several of these random strangers have wanted to scream back, "Do I look like a psychic?" None ever did. How could I not see this person was stuck behind the same eighteen-wheeler that I was? Now I sit peacefully, knowing I'm so far behind it doesn't really matter. All the frantic gestures in the world are not going to move that stalled car.

Epilogue: I write these words knowing that I am not alone. So I ask you -- when was the last time you used the word leisure in a sentence that had anything whatsoever to do with your reality? I actually looked up the word 'leisure', just to reacquaint myself with the concept. I found all kinds of words I don't use anymore --- free time, spare time, time off, plus the most interesting synonym of all - - freedom.

It struck me so, now I'm wondering if these people we now fear have stolen my freedom, or if I robbed myself of it long ago?

Money Laundering

Why does the criminal element goes to all the trouble establishing offshore bank accounts and creating legitimate businesses fronts when all *you have to do to launder money is...forget to empty your pockets?* I found twenty-seven dollars in the bottom of our washer yesterday and was so excited that you would have thought I had discovered a pot-of-gold. This leads me to a fairly obvious question. Why do we get so thrilled when we happen upon money that was ours in the first place? As soon as I spotted that money in the washer, I immediately thought to myself..."Very cool, now we can get that Chinese take-out I've been craving." It *never* even crossed my mind to put this "found" money back into the same pile of limited funds that it came from. *Where would be the fun in that?* The same principal applies to money found in old purses, what you get when you return an item and receive cash, rebate checks, refunds from cancelled policies, garage sale proceeds and money made at a consignment shop.

All of these "found" money sources have one thing in common...you paid out of one pocket to put the "new" money back into another pocket. I have thoroughly analyzed why funds from these particular sources seem like manna from heaven. My resulting rationale is very simple. This money has already been spent once. It is technically no longer available to spend again. Therefore, any proceeds from these funds would/should be outside the realm of our budget. My dad and my husband both heartily disagree with my unorthodox theory...as would any accountant, financial planner, or otherwise fiscally-sound adult.

We had decided only an hour earlier to take a pass on the Chinese take-out, making do with whatever we found in the fridge. Imagine Hugh's surprise when I told him I now had cash for take-out, but had never left our apartment. "Where did you get the cash?" he asked in a curious tone. "I found it in the washer," I explained enthusiastically. We've been married for four years now, long enough for both of us to know how and when to choose our battles. Hugh looked at me for only a few moments before replying, "OK, honey, you call them, I'll go pick it up."

Our whole goal for the last three months has been to prioritize, to downsize, to simplify our lives. Some would say we are making short-term sacrifices for long-term goals. It doesn't feel like we've given up anything that really matters. Anyone who has experienced true sacrifice will understand what I mean.

Epilogue: I would probably be more responsible with winnings from the lotto, since this would be money spent for the first time. I have a funny feeling I will never be able to prove this particular theory. So I will continue to revel in the twenty-seven dollars that comes my way just often enough to make my day. *Surprises can come in small packages...when they make you smile, well, that makes them priceless!*

Cheap Motels

Why did we have to start naming the cheap hotels/motels, "Cheap Hotel/Motel?" As a public, have we lost the ability to discern between the five star and no-star places to stay? I can recognize the no-star motels/hotels. These are where we stayed when we were traveling cross-country for family vacations. There are the same places I stayed twenty years later during college football road trips, when "room maximum" was just another edict to be ignored. They are the exactly the same today. Is someone, anyone, mistaking this no-frills look for a plush spa? I don't think so. I have faith that every American and every tourist can size up the price range of these places to stay at a glance. I think it is patronizing to put the price in the hotel/motel name.

I've been thinking about this for some time. It's on my mind right now, because I'm actually staying in a hotel at this moment. There are some common denominators in all hotels and motels, ranging from the swankiest to the cheapest. That's what I really want to talk about.

I don't care if you're paying thirty-nine dollars or two hundred and thirty-nine dollars, there is going to be a broken ice machine on your floor. You sneak out of your room (in clothing you hope never to be seen in - - or even less) to get some ice. The ice machine on your floor is empty. You find yourself scampering around the two floors above and below yours, just to get one bucket of that wonderful, easy-to-chew-hotel-ice. Meanwhile, you've propped your door open with your best shoe, because, remember, you were just running down the hall. Now you find yourself two floors down, scantily clad, praying that someone is not stealing your laptop.

More commonalities amongst all hotels: Same movies, same up-down arrows on the TV remote, same ability to order yourself a movie by mistake. They trick you on purpose, I am sure. One minute you think you are just browsing, the next minute you are staring at a screen that says, "Thank you - - your movie will begin in one minute." Whoops, no, **I don't want a movie! I was only browsing my options!** If you're really lucky, you hit the down (wrong) arrow button first and find yourself in the adult movie section when this occurs. It doesn't matter if the charges are reversed on the hotel bill when you turn in your expense account, this does not look good!

Third and final observation: The long distance telephone rate war has not made it to hotel-motel land. Any calls placed from your room to anywhere but the hotel lobby will cost you approximately five dollars a minute. So, if you forget your phone card or your cell phone has no service in that area, brace yourself upon checkout for a phone bill that could be greater than your room bill. If you are calling internationally, be prepared to spend the remaining time of your vacation in debtors' prison. Don't laugh – this is still a practice in some countries.

Epilogue: I think that all of us prefer four-star plush to bare bones. Just remember - - The towels and the TP are not always fluffier on the other side of the street.

TV War

It is a peculiar feeling to wake up each morning, trying to decide between watching the war on TV or the weather channel. *Odder still determining which one might impact me more today!* Is it because we see war and death on the made-for-TV movies and in films that this all seems so surreal? Is the monster, Saddam Hussein, somehow less real than Hitler, because he can eradicate us with a missile as opposed to a gas chamber?

I watch the demonstrators and I admire them. Not necessarily because I agree with their mantra. But because they hold a passion driven out of me by conflicting information and the dismal reality of our national and personal economics. When did my passion disappear? Have I become numb to current events, including war, by the seemingly endless debate on public and international policy? Does this news coverage strike anyone else as a terrible invasion of military and personal privacy?

I am certain of this: there are millions of people all over the globe, who loathe us for reasons I am not able to fully comprehend, with explanations we are not meant to understand. We saw this hatred manifest in the tragic events of 9/11. Hatred is taught...we can see that here at home. Yet we do not loathe a nation's people. We disdain the regime that imprisons their thoughts and their minds, threatening our lives.

I wonder what the wives, children, mothers, fathers and siblings of our soldiers feel, watching the war on TV, hoping for a glimpse of their son, daughter, husband, wife, or father.

I am neither a "hawk" nor a "dove". I am a patriot. I believe there are many things worth fighting for, worth dying for even. If an invader landed on US soil, threatening our personal liberty and our nation's freedom, I would hope I would have the fortitude to fight. I would hope that, at the very least, I could muster the anger that I felt when our neighbor dumped his lawn cuttings on our lawn. I don't want to stop caring about situations that end with our property line. *What I fear most is my own complacency.*

119

Epilogue: America, with all of its might, is still a young nation. It is our nation's youth, in that far away desert, who are prepared to make the ultimate sacrifice, to ensure that we are safe from harm's way. God bless our President and our military leaders. Provide them with wisdom, our troops with courage for battle and the fear that will keep them safe. And God bless the innocent victims of this war.

I chose the weather channel. *I cannot watch this TV war -- I feel I somehow missed the beginning and am terrified at how it might end.*

Death and Taxes

T he office was painted in a dullish gray, the chair was a straight
    back and the walls were blank. As if this whole tax thing isn't
painful enough, my CPA's office resembled an interrogation room.
I was there representing our family for our first joint filing.
Naturally, Hugh's portion of this process was completely straightforward
so he did not have to attend. Like millions of Americans, Hugh had one
W2 and a couple of receipts to write off. My fiscal history in 1999
included: one fulltime job, commission from an old job, charitable
contributions in the form of a folder of receipts, three home addresses, a
name change, and a pile of business expense receipts. When I was
gathering the goods to take to this meeting, the only folder in 1999 that
was well organized was the one marked "wedding receipts." Imagine
that. My question is this; if it takes this much time and trouble to tell the
truth about your taxes, exactly how do these tax evaders pull it off? The
way I see it, you would have to know where you put something to then
know how to hide it.

Since there was nothing to read or look at, I had plenty of time to
reminisce. I recalled when I happily sat down with Hugh and established
our budget categories. We wanted a realistic picture of where our money
went so we purchased a very sophisticated accounting software. With a
simple push of a button, the incidental twenty-dollar expenditures on
household goods and clothes are grouped together and totaled. I see
now that this software was a very serious strategic error on my part as I
had taken great pains to not spare Hugh from these acquisition totals. I
would bring in the packages and place them in a holding room." My
room of choice was the laundry room as it is not a place that Hugh
frequents. Over a period of days, I would then integrate my purchases
into our household system. Because of this method, Hugh found the
final number quite shocking. He was also astonished by the sum total of
what it takes to keep my now graying hair blonde and exactly how much
we pay for the privilege of owning a pet. Yes, I made the mistake of

giving Champ, our dog, his own category as well. Imagine how warm and fuzzy Hugh feels about his step-dog realizing that vet bills exceeded our doctor bills by one hundred fifty percent. He was still reeling from the Champ total when we came upon the dry cleaning expenses. Since then, we have both taken up ironing as a hobby.

After our little reality check meeting that evening, we came up with global categories more along the lines of HIS and HERS. Hugh does see the value in making our house a home; he just doesn't want to know the exact cost of that effort. He is being left in charge of the bills, the tell-all software, and the receipts. I am certain that next year's tax filing will go more smoothly than this one.

Epilogue: The inevitability of death and taxes. One would think you wouldn't have to pay the ladder even after the former but as we all know, that just isn't so.

Home Selling Siege

Hugh and I have made the decision to sell our home. I am certain there is a lot of emotional turmoil that comes with this decision, but what house seller has the time to go there? Trying to sell one's home is like participating in a perpetual fire drill, just without the fire.

It is the constant state of readiness that is killing me. From sun-up till sundown, all cooking and eating paraphernalia must be washed and put away. There must be no mud in the "mud room", our bed must be made and the carpet freshly vacuumed. This, of course, in addition to any other mess you've created by simply living and/or working in your home. You learn to not start any project that can't be completed in thirty minutes or less. Not that I do this anyway, but baking cookies would be a great example of what one shouldn't do while trying to sell one's home.

The Bat-phone rings. "We're in your area, can we come by?" In just four showings I have learned to gauge how many ten-minute increments I need before all will be ready. Is the bathroom clean? Is the garbage empty? Have I showered? Where's the dog? Where's my husband? Is he wearing that T-shirt with the hole in it? Is the laundry done and/or hidden away?

"Sure, that's great. Just give me X minutes and we'll be out of your hair." I hang up the phone to begin running around the house like a maniac, trying to get the place ready. This flies in the face of the most important rule for emergency management, which is - - **Don't Panic!** I find myself barking out completely absurd directives to Hugh, such as "*Dry the sinks!*"

It took me a couple of weeks to reach this level of preparedness. Initially I was throwing junk in my closet, until I realized that, unlike having company, *these people would be looking in our closets*. The first couple of visitors had to overlook a master closet that looked like a storage shed. This was only if they could get beyond the dining room table, which was "Tax Central" for the shop. In short, the house was not ready for prime time.

My realtor and dear friend, Linda, also had to break the news that not everyone believes in having knick-knacks cover every available square inch of their home. She unmercifully marched around our house pointing out things that needed to be hidden or ditched. O.K. fine. But where does this stuff go? To the garage and the basement of course! I've actually had to post a disclaimer notice on the state-of-affairs in both of these gigantic, knick-knack, way-lay stations.

Epilogue: Since the "For Sale" sign went up our little family has spent a lot of quality time together - - in our van. It took Champ, our dog, and three drills to realize that we were just cruising the neighborhood and then we were all coming home. It is an unnerving experience. It takes about ten minutes for all three of us to stop shaking. The home sellers prayer is a short one, "Lord, please send us a buyer soon. Amen."

The Proverbial Last Load

Over the last several weeks, I have been preparing for our big move. I measured dozens of furniture lengths, closet widths and window heights. When taking a house and squeezing its contents into an apartment, one has to be very conscientious of what will...or won't fit...and make decisions accordingly.

It never occurred to me to measure a particular piece of furniture for the purpose of determining...*if it could actually leave the space in which it was assembled two and a half years ago!* Thus the reason why the center of my professional world, my desk, is still sitting alone, in my office at the house we just sold. It was ugly.

Three paid movers, my father-in-law and my husband Hugh, the engineer, were all spatially challenged, trying to figure out how to get this gargantuan piece of furniture out of the doorway, then down two narrow halls. At some point, I realized the labor we were paying for this male brainstorming session was costing more than the desk did in the first place. We aborted the mission at that precise moment.

This, of course, was after the desk had been shrink-wrapped, with all of my files inside because there were no more empty boxes left to dump them in! Not knowing what else to do, we just shut the door and walked away. One only reaches this phase of "I couldn't care less" during the final moments of a move. This is when you'd rather hand someone you've never even met two hundred dollars worth of frozen meat, than try to find a cooler to tote it in.

In the final phases of a move, the value of an item is determined by the following formula. Multiply the size of an item by its weight, and then divide by the number of people left to carry it. Now you know why you see mattresses left on the side of the highway...these folks did the math and it just was not worth it to them!

So you finish all but the proverbial last load. You then caravan to your new home, trying all the while to get psyched for your next role as box traffic cop. This is when you stand at the door, while the movers zoom in and out with random loads of boxes, asking you where they go.

Your goal is to get the encyclopedias and everything else dumped as close to their final resting place as possible.

Otherwise you have a weeklong "move within a move". Which is when you're scooting around boxes with your feet that weigh seventy pounds, with no dolly and no manpower in sight.

Some things made it out safely that I wish now had not. Specifically, the box marked, "cute clothes that don't fit." Apparently, our moving men had never seen a box labeled quite so truthfully. They had to take a break, they were all laughing so hard. *Thanks, guys!!*

Epilogue: Years ago, my brother Jeffrey was enlisted to help my sister, Marsha, move home from college one summer. During the unloading of her apartment, he ran across a huge box labeled, "boxes too good to throw away." **Jeff's response...***"That's what you think! "* **as he pitched them in the nearest dumpster.**

As Seen On TV

I have always had a 900 number block on my home phone, just in case I feel the urge to call a psychic. **What this does not protect me from** is the late night temptation of ordering the bizarre and unique products peddled to exhausted housewives and insomniacs at two in the morning.

From the ceiling duster to the onion-chopper and everything in-between – "The pain and suffering caused by impossible home chores will end when you buy our product!!" On this particular morning, they were speaking directly to me as they reenacted the nightmare of dragging around a fifty-pound garden hose. This is, of course, after you've practically had to wrestle the thing to the ground to remove the kinks and knots. There are mornings when I don't care if the whole yard lives or dies, by the time I finally get the sprinkler in place.

I called the 1-800 number and ordered not one, but two, fifty-foot, featherweight garden hoses. It never occurred to me that something so straightforward could end up being so complicated. It was just a hose after all - - *what could possibly go wrong?* You would think that, having been somewhat of a walking calamity for most of my forty-three years; I would know the answer to that particular question.

When I explained my hose dilemma to the very helpful telephone order person, she suggested I have the hoses express-shipped, to guarantee delivery within five days. *Of course, great idea!*

Only one of my pre-paid, light-as-a-feather hoses arrived *FOUR WEEKS* later but my enthusiasm had not waned. I unwrapped my package with the zeal of a child on Christmas morning. I was only somewhat discouraged when I took out the hose paraphernalia - - the nozzle looked suspiciously like a toy water pistol made of day-glow plastic.

Ever hopeful, I hooked up my new miracle hose to the faucet and unfurled what I deemed The Ninth Wonder of the World. I turned on the water and watched amazed as the limp, green snake filled with water and turned into a real hose. I was just about to grab my day-glow lime green "water pistol" when water began leaking from the faucet fitting. I ran to investigate what had gone wrong, when water began spewing from the hose itself. The hose then took on a life of its own, curling and dancing as the water pressure built up and several new leaks sprung. I finally had the good sense to turn the water off at the faucet, but not before I was completely drenched.

It is moments and experiences like this when I question whether or not gardening is really my forte. Like every hobby I fantasize about mastering, there is always a kink, once the plan moves from paper to practice.

Epilogue: Several days later I was shopping at one of my favorite discount stores. I spotted dozens of the hoses in a display with a giant sign that read, "As seen on TV". There were several men and women eyeing them with interest and I felt it was my civic duty to tell them about my "hose encounter". The women immediately removed the box from their shopping carts and the men looked at me like I was nuts and, hurriedly pushed their carts away. Reality TV is big time these days! Just remember that the reality stops when the commercials start.

Pride Cometh Before the Fall

Knowing I would be traveling quite a bit with my new job, I had gone to a decent amount of trouble and expense to acquire a several new outfits. They were color coordinated, as well as suitable for most any occasion. My new chic ensembles took the place of my previous approach to packing...which was to throw anything that fit into my bag...and pray that it worked!

I began my journey as a born-again traveler last Monday, methodically placing my new clothes and matching shoes in my hanging bag with an inordinate amount of care. Even my undergarments were carefully chosen, as this is a category that can derail even the most impressive business attire. Any woman, who has only a black bra and white shirt left at the end of a trip, knows what I mean.

Being rather new to the whole concept of "less is more" in relationship to packing, I took inventory several times. Then I allowed myself to close my bag, declaring myself ready for anything. I was very pleased with myself. My life experiences have taught me self-pride is always the precursor for disaster in my world; I didn't need a crystal ball to predict how the rest of the week would go.

Sure enough, my ego was shattered on day two, when my friend and colleague offered to iron my new jacket for me. I won't quote Ruth directly, but she advised me in a very colorful manner that my day was falling apart...before it even began. It seems that somehow, someway, I was able to pay for my clothes in full...*and yet still be the proud owner of the store's security tag!*

The tag couldn't have been located in a discrete spot like my pocket; that would have been too easy! This huge tag, filled with the catch-a-thief inkwell, was located squarely on my backside. Like most women, I have features I don't mind drawing attention to...but I assure you this is not one of them. I considered getting in a cab in my morning muumuu to have the tag removed, but assumed they would need a receipt to prove I had purchased the jacket. I thought about having Husband Hugh fax me the receipt...*until I realized I hadn't told him I had bought the jacket in the first place!*

I was upset, but only mildly so as with my new and improved packing plan I had choices! I went to put my pants on with another shirt. Imagine my dismay when the zipper would not go up. Again, somehow, someway, the dry cleaners had pressed the pants so well *the zipper "teeth" were melted*, rendering the Plan B pants useless, as well. These two ridiculous scenarios left me no choice but to put on my *Day 3* outfit with no pantyhose. My only option was to use the knee-highs I was going to wear with my pants...and beg my friend, Ruth, to just shoot me, if any point during the day you could see them from the audience. I'm certain there is something less becoming than seeing knee-high hose clinging tightly to a woman's calf but I couldn't tell you what that something is at this moment.

Epilogue: I've found while presenting a subject as complex as software, one should concentrate on the topic at hand. For that entire day, I no longer cared if anyone liked our product. I was focused only on keeping my knee-highs above my hemline. "Pride cometh before the fall"...always.

To Rent or to Borrow, That is the Question

Thank goodness my friend Betsy isn't a video rental establishment or I would owe her something in the neighborhood of ten thousand dollars in late fees. You see, I borrowed the Sandra Dee movie, *If a Man Answers* from Bets in 1987 and have yet to return it to her. Am seriously wishing she had a drop box that I could put it in so that she wouldn't know who has had her movie for the last sixteen years.

I found the Sandra Dee flick in a most unlikely place: a filing cabinet in my office where it must have fallen into years ago. Every few years since 1987 I would come across this tape and say to myself, "Sharon, how rude! You really need to give this back to Betsy!" I then take the tape and put it somewhere where I won't forget and then I do...forget it that is.

Ironic that I would happen upon this VCR tape today as I am debating whether or not I want to rent a movie tonight knowing the late fee that awaits me there. We owe almost twenty bucks on the last movie we rented and never watched. This is such a pitiful waste of money that not even I can stomach it... and I can stomach a lot where wasted money is concerned!

It's hard enough to remember to return the movies we do watch much less these that just sit on top of the entertainment center for a week or two. You see, when you don't actually see the film it never enters your thought pattern again. You can pass it by every morning and every evening and think, "oh my gosh, someone needs to return that movie." You put it on top of the clothes that you're taking to the dry cleaner and then tell yourself the great movie rental lie; *"I'll keep it one more night and watch it before I take it back."* The movie is then returned to its previous dust-free spot where it sits for another three days unwatched.

After a week of this ridiculous game, I become too annoyed with myself to even watch the movie. It doesn't matter if the film walked away with five Oscars. As an example of my perfectly illogical logic I then say to myself, "That stupid movie isn't worth twenty bucks...I'm not watching it!"

I am bitter but alas, I will go to the video store and pay my debt to society. I mean, even the library sticks you with a late charge. I will comb the New Release racks as I have a thousand times before wondering...what the heck was the name of that film my buddy Roy told me to rent? And I will ask myself the following question: Do these places actually forecast in their budget how many idiots like me keep movies for a week after they are due? Of course they do.

Epilogue: Bets, if you're reading this column could you please cut me some slack on the late fee? Better still, let's have a slumber party and watch this classic chick-flick together like we used to back when I borrowed it from you. There is nothing better in this world during stressful times than an old friend and an old movie.

Never, Ever 'No-Show' Your Hairdresser

As ridiculously superficial as this may sound, it is true. *Most women would quicker cancel their annual with their doctor than "no-show" their hairdresser!* Women today have more in common with Samson than Delilah! Our power and our strength are sometimes completely based on whether or not we're having a "Good Hair Day". I have no idea when the female sense-of-self transferred to the top of our heads. It was sometime after men stopped wearing wigs...and before the advent of hair rollers.

This theory has been borne out. My colleague and dear friend, Ruth, and I have had to just rearrange our entire lives for our new jobs. We have canceled and rescheduled dates with husbands, family and friends and spent many late hours playing catch up on our personal lives.

Note that only once in three months, have either of us dared to give up our space on our hairdresser's calendar. It was Ruth's appointment, thank goodness! A sought-after hairdresser makes no apology when they can't fit you in for another month. This punishment period is imposed so you will think twice before you dare leave them with an empty chair again. Ruth's cancellation was five weeks ago...*her hairdresser was finally able to squeeze her in yesterday!*

Ruth is a new woman today. Since I couldn't tell the difference, I'm able to admit, maybe, just maybe, some of the female hair obsession is a little over the top. I don't even want to get into the feminist perspective on all of this, but I will mention male-pattern-baldness is perhaps the great equalizer.

I've been reading a book, *The Tipping Point.* It theorizes little things can make a big difference and that all situations in life have that defining moment, when the circumstances suddenly change. The book is fairly thought provoking so I'm certain the author, Mr. Gladwell, would be appalled to know I'm now including hairstyles in the class of "Things That Tip".

Whether fact or fiction, women believe our hair looks great for two weeks...decent for another two...then "tips" into a state of disaster. You can literally go from bouncy to wilting hair in what seems like hours.

From natural blonde (OK, *it was natural,* once upon a time) to gray roots in a day.

Yesterday's blow-and-go cut becomes today's flattop look. And all the round brush techniques in the world aren't going to save us. People think investing in the stock market is risky. ***Risk is going to a new stylist two days before a big event!***

Epilogue: When women end up in this "Bad Hair" zone, we look to those around us for affirmation that we can go out in the world without a baseball cap on. Occasionally, we even ask the men in our lives, who *still* make the mistake of assuming that we're looking for an honest assessment. When will men learn? The right answer to any question beginning with, *"Does my ...? or, Do I ...?",* is simply -- *"Honey, you look fabulous!"*

If we wanted the truth, we would call a girlfriend or, better still...our hairdresser!

A Bushel and a Peck

David, my oldest nephew tried to negotiate a deal with me. He would agree to voluntarily give me a hug good night, *IF* I would refrain from kissing him and tucking him in. I told it was my job, as his Aunt, to bestow upon him some annoying sign of affection whenever I saw him. He rolled his eyes, snickered, and proceeded to pull the covers tightly over his head. His younger brother, Jonathan, lay giggling on the bottom bunk, peeking out from under his blankets. I grabbed his little face between my hands and kissed his adorable cheek. Jonathan ducked under his covers and mumbled, "Aunt Sharon, I'm too big for you to kiss me goodnight!" Yet his grin told me differently. When Jonathan offers a hug in exchange for a kiss, I will know that he, too, is leaving childhood to become a young man.

My own Aunt Dorothy used to do the cheek-pinching routine with all of us. She would grab a big hunk of the side of your face between her thumb and forefinger, smile, then grit her teeth and tell us how cute we were and just how much she loved us. "Great," we'd think to ourselves, "Now just let go of my face...you're hurting me!" Her sister, my Aunt Ruth, is a cheek-pincher too. My grandmother, their mother, was an upper-arm-grabber, and her son, my Father, is a bear hugger. Clearly, the subliminal message of my youth was "Love Hurts."

My Mother's "TLC" manifested itself in a far more vocal way. She would tiptoe into our bedroom every morning singing (and I use the term loosely), "I love you a bushel and a peck...". We would moan loudly; we would plug our ears; we would roll over to muffle the sound of her shrill voice. Yet we would anticipate and depend on this annoying ritual just as we did the rising of the sun.

If I had known, while receiving all those pinches, hugs and songs, that when you hit 18 you enter *affection deprivation*, I would have stored up for the winter, so to speak. I remember when, like my nephews, I reached the age when I was too old to want a hug and to young to know that I needed one. It was that same awkward age when I still wanted my

135

stuffed animals nestled around me, but knew it was time they took their place in the attic.

Epilogue: Maybe we all let go too soon? Which is why, perhaps, when I felt so sad last week, I had an overwhelming urge to do laundry at my Mother's house. She must have sensed the real need, because although she spent two hours babbling about nothing, when I was leaving she put her arms around me and gently rocked me back and forth.

Let's face it; it was the hug that I drove eighteen miles for, not the load of wash. So in a world where you can't count on much, *I know my Mom still loves me "a bushel and a peck"* ---- and I'll tell you what, **I'm awfully, awfully glad.**

Epilogue

The stories inside *Write Like You Don't Need the Money* were written because life can be absolutely hilarious, completely absurd, and sometimes poignant...sort of like reality TV without the cameras. I write my weekly column, *Off the Cuff*, not only because it pays my dry cleaning bill but also because it gives me great joy. The time I spend with myself each week to sit back and laugh out loud at my own insanity has been a real blessing in my life.

My mom taught me that the ability to laugh at oneself could get a person through some rough times. She, my husband Hugh, my precious family, and countless friends have provided the material for my column over the years. These people who I love have given me insight into their un-varnished selves and lovingly held the mirror for me to see myself for who I really am, which by the by, isn't always easy.

I wouldn't change a thing about my life. Because if one moment were altered then I might have missed out on one of these "characters"...the people in my life who have made me rich in the only way that matters to me.

The characters and events in this book are real. Any similarity to real persons in your own lives is the reason why humor is the only true universal language. Thank God for laughter.

Peace,
Sharon Kuhn Young

Printed in the United States
1436100001B/298-417